Level 5

Read and Succeed:
Comprehension

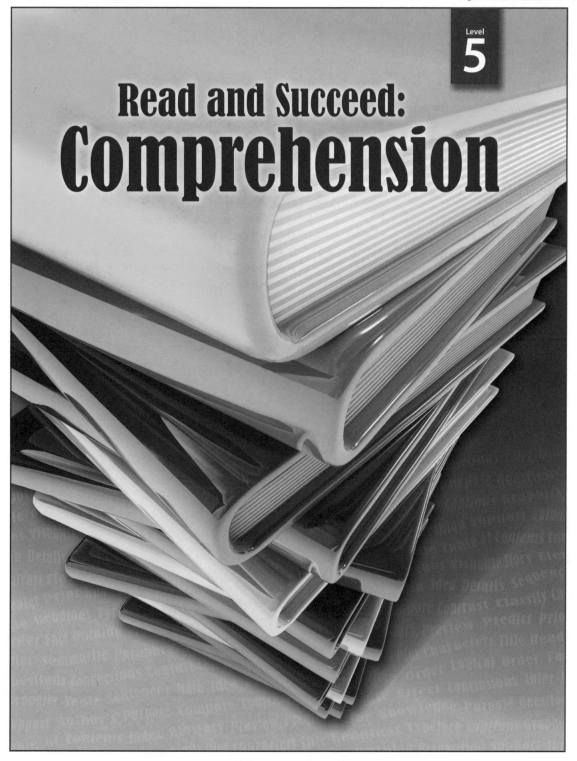

Consultant

Debra J. Housel, M.S.Ed.

SHELL EDUCATION

Contributing Authors

Lisa Greathouse

Stephanie Paris

Greg Timmons

Publishing Credits

Dona Herweck Rice, *Editor-in-Chief*; Lee Aucoin, *Creative Director*; Don Tran, *Print Production Manager;* Timothy J. Bradley, *Illustration Manager;* Conni Medina, M.A.Ed., *Editorial Director*; Kristy Stark, M.A.Ed., *Editor*; Stephanie Reid, *Cover Designer;* Robin Erickson, *Interior Layout Designer;* Corinne Burton, M.S.Ed., *Publisher*

Copyright 2004 McREL. www.mcrel.org/standards-benchmarks.

Shell Education

5301 Oceanus Drive
Huntington Beach, CA 92649-1030
http://www.shelleducation.com

ISBN 978-1-4258-0728-3

©2010 Shell Educational Publishing, Inc.

Table of Contents

Introduction

Comprehension is the goal of every reading task. The *Read and Succeed: Comprehension* series can help lay the foundation of comprehension skills that are essential for a lifetime of learning. The series was written specifically to provide the purposeful practice students need in order to succeed in reading comprehension. The more students practice, the more confident and capable they can become.

Why You Need This Book

- **It is standards based.** The skill practice pages are aligned to the Mid-continent Research for Education and Learning (McREL) standards. (See page 7.)
- **It has focused lessons.** Each practice page covers a key comprehension skill. Skills are addressed multiple times to provide several opportunities for mastery.
- **It employs advanced organization.** Having students encounter the question page first gives them a "heads up" when they approach the text, thereby enhancing comprehension and promoting critical-thinking abilities.
- **It has appropriate reading levels.** All passages have a grade level calculated based on the Shell Education leveling system, which was developed under the guidance of Dr. Timothy Rasinski, along with the staff at Shell Education.
- **It has an interactive whiteboard-compatible Teacher Resource CD.** This can be used to enhance instruction and support literacy skills.

How to Use This Book

First, determine what sequence will best benefit your students. Work through the book in order (as the skills become progressively more difficult) to cover all key skills. For reinforcement of specific skills, select skills as needed.

Then determine what instructional setting you will use. See below for suggestions for a variety of instructional settings:

Whole-Class or Small-Group Instruction	Independent Practice or Centers	Homework
Read and discuss the Skill Focus. Write the name of the skill on the board.	Create a folder for each student. Include a copy of the selected skill practice page and passage.	Give each student a copy of the selected skill practice page and passage.
Read and discuss responses to each question. Read the text when directed (as a group, in pairs, or individually).	Have students complete the skill practice page. Remind them to begin by reading the Skill Focus and to read the passage when directed.	Have students complete the skill practice page. Remind them to begin by reading the Skill Focus and to read the passage when directed.
Read and discuss the Critical Thinking question. Allow time for discussion before having students write their responses.	Collect the skill practice pages and check students' answers. Or, provide each student with a copy of the answer key (pages 138–149).	Collect the skill practice pages and check students' answers. Or, provide each student with a copy of the answer key (pages 138–149).

Research Support for the
Read and Succeed: Comprehension Series

Comprehension is the ability to derive meaning from text. It is critically important not only for the development of children's reading skills but also for students' abilities to obtain a complete education. The National Reading Panel (2000) states that comprehension is an active process that requires an intentional interaction between the reader and the text. A reader must engage in problem-solving thinking processes in order to relate the ideas represented in print to his or her own knowledge and experiences and build mental images to store in memory.

Teaching students to use specific strategies can improve their comprehension. To some degree, readers acquire such strategies informally. However, the National Reading Panel confirmed that explicit instruction in comprehension strategies is highly effective in enhancing understanding. That's why the *Read and Succeed: Comprehension* series was created: to make teaching comprehension strategies simple and time efficient. This book teaches specific strategies students can use to help them understand what they are reading.

Having students know in advance the questions they will be asked helps them to attend to the material. It gives them a focus as they read. It helps them to look for clues and to identify information they will need to remember. But most importantly, it allows them to organize information in their minds, building neural pathways that will be used again and again. Essentially, having a focus as they read teaches children how to think. This is why the skill practice page always appears before the reading passage in *Read and Succeed: Comprehension.*

Teaching a combination of reading comprehension techniques is the most effective approach for instruction. When students use strategies appropriately, they can improve their recall, question answering, question generation, and summarization of texts. Also, used in combination, these techniques can improve results in standardized comprehension tests. Yet teaching reading comprehension strategies to students at all grade levels can be complex. The *Read and Succeed: Comprehension* series was designed to make this process straightforward. Each book contains 65 lessons. Each lesson has a specific focus to concentrate on an important reading skill for a fiction or a nonfiction text. Step by step, students will learn the grade-level-appropriate skills they need to read and understand a wide variety of texts.

Each skill activity is independent; they need not be done in a certain order. However, it is in students' best interest to complete all of the activities. Using the *Read and Succeed: Comprehension* series will save you time and effort while simultaneously providing students with the vital skills needed to achieve 21st century comprehension and critical-thinking skills.

National Institute of Child Health and Human Development. 2000. *Report of the National Reading Panel. Teaching children to read: An evidence-based assessment of the scientific research literature on reading and its implications for reading instruction* (NIH Publication No. 00-4769). Washington, DC: U.S. Government Printing Office.

Standards Correlations

Shell Education is committed to producing educational materials that are research and standards based. In this effort, we have correlated all of our products to the academic standards of all 50 states, the District of Columbia, and the Department of Defense Dependent Schools.

How to Find Standards Correlations

To print a customized correlation report of this product for your state, visit our website at **www.shelleducation.com** and follow the on-screen directions. If you require assistance in printing correlation reports, please contact Customer Service at 1-877-777-3450.

Purpose and Intent of Standards

The No Child Left Behind legislation mandates that all states adopt academic standards that identify the skills students will learn in kindergarten through grade twelve. While many states had already adopted academic standards prior to NCLB, the legislation set requirements to ensure the standards were detailed and comprehensive.

Standards are designed to focus instruction and guide adoption of curricula. Standards are statements that describe the criteria necessary for students to meet specific academic goals. They define the knowledge, skills, and content students should acquire at each level. Standards are also used to develop standardized tests to evaluate students' academic progress.

Teachers are required to demonstrate how their lessons meet state standards. State standards are used in development of all of our products, so educators can be assured they meet the academic requirements of each state.

McREL Compendium

We use the Mid-continent Research for Education and Learning (McREL) Compendium to create standards correlations. Each year, McREL analyzes state standards and revises the compendium. By following this procedure, McREL is able to produce a general compilation of national standards. Each lesson in this product is based on one or more McREL standards. The chart on the following page lists each standard taught in this product and the page numbers for the corresponding lessons.

McREL Correlations Chart

Skills	Skill Focus and Page Numbers
Previews text	*Preview*, 8–9, 10–11
Establishes a purpose for reading	*Set a Purpose*, 20–21, 22–23; *Ask Questions*, 24–25, 26–27
Makes, confirms, and revises predictions	*Predict*, 12–13, 14–15; *Visualize*, 36–37, 38–39
Uses a variety of context clues to decode unknown words	*Context Clues*, 32–33, 34–35
Uses word reference materials (e.g., glossary) to determine the meaning, pronunciation, and derivations of unknown words	*Glossary*, 134–135, 136–137
Understands author's purpose or point of view	*Author's Purpose*, 94–95, 96–97
Uses reading skills and strategies to understand and interpret a variety of literary texts	*Story Elements*, 40–41, 42–43
Understands the basic concept of plot	*Plot*, 44–45, 46–47
Understands elements of character development	*Characters*, 48–49, 50–51
Makes connections between characters or events in a literary work and people or events in his or her own life	*Make Connections*, 28–29, 30–31
Uses reading skills and strategies to understand and interpret a variety of informational texts	*Fact and Opinion*, 86–87, 88–89; *Classify*, 102–103, 104–105; *Draw Conclusions*, 110–111, 112–113; *Infer*, 114–115, 116–117
Uses text organizers (e.g., headings, topic and summary sentences, graphic features, typeface, chapter titles) to determine the main ideas and to locate information in a text	*Titles and Headings*, 52–53, 54–55; *Typeface and Captions*, 56–57, 58–59; *Graphics*, 60–61, 62–63; *Topic Sentences*, 64–65, 66–67
Identifies the main idea and supporting details	*Main Idea*, 68–69, 70–71; *Details*, 72–73, 74–75; *Main Idea and Details*, 76–77
Uses the various parts of a book to locate information (e.g., table of contents, index)	*Table of Contents*, 126–127, 128–129; *Index*, 130–131, 132–133
Summarizes and paraphrases information in texts	*Summarize*, 118–119, 120–121; *Paraphrase*, 122–123, 124–125
Uses prior knowledge and experience to understand and respond to new information	*Prior Knowledge*, 16–17, 18–19
Understands structural patterns or organization in informational texts (e.g., chronological, logical, or sequential order; compare and contrast; cause and effect; proposition and support)	*Chronological Order*, 78–79, 80–81; *Logical Order*, 82–83, 84–85; *Proposition and Support*; 90–91, 92–93 *Compare and Contrast*, 98–99, 100–101; *Cause and Effect*, 106–107, 108–109

Preview

Looking at the title, pictures, and headings before you read helps you to get ready to understand the text.

1. Preview the text. What do you already know about the Egyptian pyramids?

   _____

   _____

2. Read the text. Why do you think the students measured the sides of the Great Pyramid at Giza?

   _____

   _____

3. Write two facts that you learned about the pyramids from the text.

   _____

   _____

   _____

   _____

Critical Thinking

How did previewing the text help you to understand it when you read it?

   _____

   _____

   _____

THE TRIP OF A LIFETIME

The students of the American International School were excited. They had worked hard raising money for this trip. They had washed cars, sold magazine subscriptions, and collected cans and bottles. Now they were flying to Cairo to tour the pyramids of Egypt!

Before the trip, the students had studied the pyramids in school. They learned about the pharaohs, the ancient kings of Egypt who ruled Egypt nearly 5,000 years ago. The Egyptians considered the pharaohs to be living gods. The pyramids were constructed as tombs for the pharaohs. Often it took a pharaoh's whole lifetime for his pyramid to be erected.

On the first day of the trip, the students went to the Great Pyramid in Giza. It was built for the Pharaoh Khufu around 2550 B.C. The Great Pyramid is the tallest in the world. Originally, it was 480 feet (146.3 m) tall. Due to erosion, it is now approximately 450 feet (137.2 m) tall. The students were amazed by the precision that was used to build the pyramid with the primitive technology available at that time. They measured all four sides of the Great Pyramid. They found each side to be 750 feet (228.6 m) long.

No one knows how the ancient Egyptians built these massive structures. Each stone in the pyramid weighs as much as four tons. Historians believe the Egyptians hadn't yet discovered the wheel. They theorize that the ancient Egyptians slid the stones on giant sleds over great distances and pulled the stones up ramps. It was such a slow process that thousands of slaves worked for decades on each pyramid.

When the students returned to school, they prepared presentations. Then they held an assembly and invited the community. Everyone was impressed by how much the students had learned.

Preview

Looking at the title, pictures, and headings before you read helps you to get ready to understand the text.

1. Preview the text. Name two people who will be mentioned in the text.

    _____   _____

2. Scan the text for other names. Write them below.

    _____   _____

3. Read the text. Then number the sentences in the correct order from first to last (1–4).

    _____ Mark Antony kills himself.

    _____ Cleopatra becomes the queen of Egypt.

    _____ Octavian defeats the Egyptians.

    _____ Julius Caesar falls in love with Cleopatra.

Critical Thinking

How did previewing the text help you to understand it when you read it?

_____

_____

_____

CLEOPATRA: QUEEN OF EGYPT

A carving of Cleopatra, Queen of Egypt, on the side of an ancient Egyptian ruin

Cleopatra is one of the most famous women in history. She lived from 69 to 30 B.C. She was beautiful and ambitious. At the age of 17, she became the queen of Egypt.

At the time Cleopatra ruled Egypt, Julius Caesar was the emperor of Rome. In 48 B.C., he visited Egypt. He fell in love with Cleopatra. When Caesar returned to Rome, Cleopatra traveled with him. But then Caesar was murdered. Cleopatra returned to Egypt alone.

To increase her power, she married a Roman general named Mark Antony. Antony was expected to become the new emperor of Rome. Soon, he started giving away Roman land to his wife. This angered a Roman general named Octavian. He declared war on Antony and Cleopatra. In a major sea battle, Octavian defeated the Egyptians. Antony killed himself. Cleopatra realized that she had lost her power. So, she took her own life—by deliberately letting a poisonous snake bite her.

Predict

Look for clues to help you guess what is coming next in a text. Answer the first four questions before you read the text.

1. Look at the title and picture. Predict Diego Rivera's profession.

   _____

2. Do you think this text will be fiction or nonfiction? Explain.

   _____

   _____

3. What do you think the word *eccentric* means?

   _____

4. Scan the text. Is Diego Rivera still alive? How do you know?

   _____

5. Read the text. Were your predictions correct? Explain.

   _____

   _____

   _____

Critical Thinking

How did making predictions help you to understand what you read?

_____

_____

_____

Diego Rivera, An Eccentric Artist

Suppose someone asks you to paint a picture. "All right," you think. "No problem. I can fill the canvas pretty easily." But what if the picture you are asked to paint is three stories high, two city blocks long, and one block wide? In other words, a total of 17,000 square feet (1,579 sq m)! Most people would be overwhelmed by the request. But not Diego Rivera.

Diego Rivera (1886–1957) was one of modern Mexico's most famous painters. When he was asked to paint this huge mural, he did not hesitate. He knew he could do it. During his life, Rivera painted 124 frescos that showed Mexican life, history, and social problems. A fresco is a painting on wet plaster.

Rivera had to plan ahead and sketch what he planned to paint. He used a special plaster that had a specific amount of lime. He used special watercolors, too.

First, Rivera's aides would apply all but the final layer of plaster. Next, they used sharp tools to dig the outlines of Rivera's sketches into the plaster. Then, they made a mixture of lime and marble dust and spread this over the outline in a thin layer. As soon as this layer was firm—but not dry—Rivera began to paint.

Every morning, his paints had to be freshly mixed. The pigments were ground by hand and mixed on a slab of marble. Rivera would paint as long as there was daylight. He refused to paint under artificial light since it would change how the colors looked.

Sometimes, Rivera would say that what he had painted that day was not good enough. Then he would insist that all the plaster be scraped off so he could start again! It took Rivera years to finish, but this mural is thought to be one of the greatest in the world. The man himself is considered to be the greatest Mexican artist of the twentieth century.

One of Rivera's colorful wall murals

Predict

Look for clues to help you guess what is coming next in a text. Answer the first two questions before you read the story.

1. Look at the title and picture. Do you think this text will be fiction or nonfiction? Explain.

   _____

   _____

2. What do you think the word *disfigured* means?

   _____

3. Read the story. Why does Moonlight keep her face hidden beneath the bearskin?

   _____

   _____

4. Were the predictions you made in #1 and #2 correct? Explain.

   _____

   _____

   _____

Critical Thinking

Predict what will happen next in the story.

_____

_____

_____

The Mysterious Maiden

"We must see her," demanded the chief's men. "We were ordered to examine every available maiden in the territory."

The tribal leader called Moonlight from her tipi. She emerged, holding the grizzly bear skin so tightly that only her hands were visible. Her eyes were golden brown as they peered through the eyeholes of the bearskin. The chief's messengers walked all around her, longing to see her face.

"Your hands look normal," one of the chief's men said. "So why do you hide your face beneath that skin?"

Moonlight did not answer.

"Your face is deformed! You are hideous," another man cried, hoping to trick her into dropping the bearskin.

Moonlight showed no distress. Instead, she calmly stated, "No one will see my face until my wedding day. I will only marry a man who loves me for myself and not for my appearance."

"Is your face so disfigured that you cannot bear to show it?" the first man inquired kindly.

"I didn't say that. I said that the man I marry must love me for myself. He must want to marry me no matter what my face looks like," Moonlight insisted.

The second of the chief's men turned to the tribal leader. "Order her to uncover her face!"

Prior Knowledge

Whenever you read, you bring what you already know about the subject to the text. You use this prior knowledge to make sense of the new information you read.

1. Read the title. Write two things that you already know about natural forces.

   _____

   _____

2. Read the text. Give an example of gravity.

   _____

   _____

3. Give your own example of friction.

   _____

   _____

4. How did the captions work to help you to understand the text?

   _____

   _____

Critical Thinking

How did thinking about what you already knew about natural forces help you to understand this text?

   _____

   _____

   _____

May the Force Be With You!

Our world has natural forces. A force is anything that pushes or pulls to make an object move. Sir Isaac Newton said that all matter has inertia. Inertia means that any object stays still or moves in the same way until a force acts upon it. For example, a cup placed on a table will stay there until someone or something creates a force to move it. Inertia also means that a sled going down a snowy hill will keep sliding in a straight path until the person in the sled does something to change its direction or it reaches the bottom of the hill.

Inertia keeps the hockey player gliding across the ice.

You've probably heard the saying, "What goes up must come down." It is based on gravity, the force that pulls everything toward the ground. And you know that magnetic force pulls metal objects closer together or pushes them apart.

Friction is an important force, too. Friction works to slow or stop movement between any two surfaces that rub together. Without friction, a person couldn't run because once that person was moving, he or she couldn't stop. A person couldn't pick up or kick a ball because it would slip away. Hikers wear boots with deep tread to increase friction. Baseball and football players wear cleats for the same reason.

The goalie's gloves apply friction to the ball, and gravity will bring her back down to the ground.

A lack of friction lets things slide. Any smooth surface, such as a kitchen counter, has less friction than a rough surface, such as a brick. Sometimes a lack of friction is good, and other times it's bad. Since snow has little friction, skiers can glide on it. Cyclists oil the gears on their bikes to make the wheels spin faster. Wet pavement also has little friction. This may cause a car to slide off the road or hit another car.

Drag is a similar force. Drag is the force of air or water slowing down the things that move through them. To reduce drag, engineers design jets and cars to be aerodynamic. Then the object slices through the air, letting it move faster. Fish have sleek bodies that can move efficiently through water. People design racing boats to do the same thing.

The swim cap allows the swimmer to glide through the water faster.

Prior Knowledge

Whenever you read, you bring what you already know about the subject to the text. You use this prior knowledge to make sense of the new information you read.

1. Read the title. Write two facts that you already know about electricity.

    _____

    _____

2. Write two facts that you already know about magnets or magnetism.

    _____

    _____

3. Read the text. Tell about a time when you experienced static electricity.

    _____

    _____

4. What metal is affected by a magnet?_____

5. Name an item in your home to which a magnet is attracted.

    _____

Critical Thinking

Think about a clothes dryer. What kind(s) of electricity may be related to it?

_____

_____

_____

NATURAL FORCES: ELECTRICITY AND MAGNETISM

Electricity

An electrical current is the flow of electrons from one place to another. An electrical circuit is what allows the current to flow. A circuit is a closed loop of conducting material such as copper. Electricity flows along it.

There are two types of electricity: current and static. Shuffle your feet across a carpet. Then touch your friend's hand. You may both feel a small shock. This shock is a tiny jolt of static electricity. Why does this happen? Electricity is at rest until it is able to move. You move the electrons from one surface to the other when you shuffle your feet on the carpet. This gives one surface a positive charge and the other surface a negative charge. The difference in charges is called a *potential difference*. When you touch your friend's hand, the jolt you feel is the electrons moving from one hand to the other. This evens out the potential difference and makes both surfaces neutral again.

Current electricity is like a river that runs in a circle. The electrons are always moving. To see how that works, we need to understand magnets.

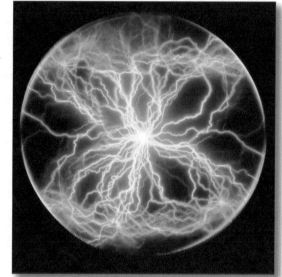

plasma ball

Magnetism

Magnets have an invisible force. This force only affects some things. Iron is one of them. Magnetic forces can move a heavy piece of iron without anything ever touching the metal.

Magnetism can only reach so far, though. The reach of a magnet is called its *magnetic field*. Magnetic forces only occur within the field.

The first magnets were found in nature. Scientists began to wonder if they could make artificial ones. One scientist found a way. In 1820, Hans Oersted placed a compass near an electrical current. He saw that the needle on the compass moved. The current had made a magnetic field. Oersted studied this some more. He found that all electrical currents have magnetic fields.

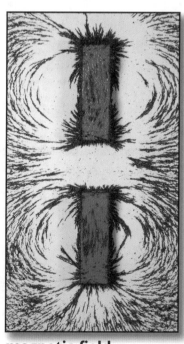

magnetic field

Set a Purpose

Before you read, ask yourself a question about the text based on the pictures or the title. Then read to find the answer. Having a purpose will help you to get more out of what you read.

1. Look at the title and pictures. Turn the title into a question.

   _____

2. Write a question that you hope the text will answer.

   _____

   _____

3. Read the text. Answer the question you wrote in #1.

   _____

   _____

4. Write one fact that you learned about volcanoes from the text.

   _____

   _____

Critical Thinking

Did the text answer your second question? If not, how can you find the answer?

_____

_____

_____

Unseen Volcanoes Build New Land

No one has ever seen some of the world's biggest volcanoes. Why not? They lie far below the sea! Earth's biggest mountain range zigzags all over the ocean floor. Every day, at least one of its volcanoes erupts, causing hot lava to pour out onto the sea floor. The ocean's cold water cools the lava, turning it into rock. Layers of this rock build up. If it reaches above the ocean's surface, it forms an island.

Hawaii and Iceland are volcanic islands. Hawaii is still growing. Its active volcanoes still erupt, and their lava adds more land.

The world's newest volcanic island appeared in 1963 near Iceland. Sailors saw a huge cloud of smoke and steam. They moved their ship closer and witnessed the birth of a new island. This island kept growing for the next three and a half years. Its name is Surtsey.

Even lava that doesn't reach the sea's surface changes land. Over a long time, the lava on the ocean floor expands and pushes on the continents. This causes them to move a little bit. Each of Earth's seven continents moves from one to three inches (2.5–7.62 cm) a year. This means that Earth's surface is always changing. A million years ago, Earth looked different than it does today. A million years from now, it will have changed again.

Hot lava flows across land.

Cooled lava turns into rock.

Set a Purpose

Before you read, ask yourself a question about the text based on the pictures or the title. Then read to find the answer. Having a purpose will help you to get more out of what you read.

1. Look at the title and pictures. Turn the title into a question.

    _____

2. Write another question that you hope the text will answer.

    _____

    _____

3. Read the text. Answer the question you wrote in #1.

    _____

    _____

4. Write one fact that you learned about Niagara Falls.

    _____

    _____

Critical Thinking

Did the text answer your second question? If not, how can you find the answer?

_____

_____

_____

Niagara Falls

Niagara Falls is part of the Niagara River. This river forms a part of the border between the United States and Canada. Niagara Falls has two parts: the Horseshoe Falls and the American Falls. Canada owns the U-shaped Horseshoe Falls. More water flows over Niagara than any other falls in the world. Millions of people visit the Falls each year.

Niagara Falls started out as river rapids. Over time, the rushing water wore away the rock of the riverbed. Different kinds of rock erode at different rates. Hard dolomite covered soft layers of limestone, sandstone, and shale. The rushing water tore away the softer rock. The hard layer was left sticking out like a shelf. Water fell over this shelf. The Falls were born!

Twelve thousand years ago, Niagara Falls was seven miles (11.2 km) downstream. Every year, more rock wore away. This made the Falls move back about three feet (1 m) each year. Slowly, the Falls moved upstream, leaving behind a deep gorge.

During the early 1900s, people started diverting water from the river above the Falls. This water flows into a power plant and makes electricity. The water is released back into the Niagara River below the Falls. As the demand for electrical power has increased, more water has been taken. Less water going over the Falls means less erosion. Now each year, the American Falls moves back about an inch (2.5 cm). Much more water goes over the Horseshoe Falls. It erodes at least 3 inches (7.6 cm) per year.

Right below the Horseshoe Falls, the water has worn a hole as deep as the Falls is high! When the lower rock layers wear away enough, the upper ledge will fall. Since this could be dangerous, scientists keep track of the Falls' edges. They blast away unstable edges so that they won't fall when people are standing on them.

Horseshoe Falls in Canada

American Falls in the United States

Ask Questions

Before you read, ask yourself, "What questions do I have about this topic? What do I hope to learn?" Then, as you read, look for the answers.

1. Look at the title and picture. What do you think this text will be about?

    _____

    _____

2. Read the text.   What was the question that Sarah asked her teacher?

    _____

3. What question did Sarah ask the principal?

    _____

4. Why do you think the principal agreed?

    _____

5. If you were the reporter, what question would you ask?

    _____

    _____

Critical Thinking

Did you like how this text was written in a question-and-answer format? Explain why or why not.

_____

_____

_____

School Website

Reporter: Thanks for talking to Alcott Community News about your school website.

Sarah: No problem. I can't wait to see my name in the newspaper!

Reporter: So, why did you start this new website for Alcott Middle School?

Sarah: Three months ago, my mom was complaining about how she never hears about the days we're dismissed early until after the fact. She works late and sometimes she has to ask our neighbor at the last minute to pick me up after school. It happened several times, and she was frustrated that there wasn't better notification from the school.

Reporter: Didn't your school already have a website with that information?

Sarah: Well, yes—and no. We had a website. But there wasn't much information on it, and nobody was in charge of keeping it up to date.

Reporter: How did you get involved?

Sarah: I asked my teacher if our class could take over updating the school calendar. That seemed pretty easy.

Reporter: Was it?

Sarah: Yeah, and it was kind of fun. So then we asked the principal if we could redo the whole site. He said okay, so we went to work. We discovered websites that taught us how to make our site look better and added more hot links that people could click to get more information about a subject. We posted photos from rallies and basketball games, and our class even started a blog about what's going on at school. Then we persuaded the teachers to create their own pages.

Reporter: So what's next?

Sarah: A few friends and I started a small Web design business. We're asking schools if they'll hire us to set up a site like the one we created.

Reporter: Wow! That's pretty enterprising for a 13-year-old.

Sarah: I guess so. But it doesn't seem like work when you're doing something you enjoy.

Ask Questions

Before you read, ask yourself, "What questions do I have about this topic? What do I hope to learn?" Then, as you read, look for the answers.

1. Look at the title and picture. What do you think this text will be about?

   _____

2. In the first column of the chart, write a question that you have before reading the text. Leave room beneath it to write the answer.

Question Before Reading	Question After Reading

3. Read the text. Fill in the answer to your question in the first column.

4. In the second column of the chart, write a question that you still have. Leave room beneath it to write the answer.

How will you find the answer to the question you wrote in the second column of the chart?

_____

_____

_____

Our Energetic World

Did you know that energy makes the world go round? It makes clouds move across the sky. It lets the trees grow taller. It helps birds to fly, feed, and build nests. The bus in which you rode to school used energy to get you there.

Almost all the energy used on Earth comes from the sun. The sun is a giant ball of hot gases with a lot of energy. That energy travels to Earth through heat and light radiation. The sun creates so much energy that it is always shooting out photons. Photons are tiny packets of energy. They rush through space until they arrive at Earth.

Some photons hit air molecules in Earth's atmosphere. Those air molecules become warmer. The air on the side of the planet facing the sun heats up more than the side facing away. Hot air expands while cold air contracts. So, the hot air moves by spreading out toward where the cold air is shrinking. This is what causes wind to blow.

Photons also hit water molecules in the oceans and other water bodies. These molecules become warmer, too. Some of them heat up so much that they evaporate. Since they are warm, they rise into the atmosphere. They float until they hit a layer of cold air. Then they condense into water vapor and form clouds.

Other photons hit the chlorophyll molecules stored in tree leaves. Those molecules grab the energy in the photons. They use the energy to make food that nourishes the tree. This lets the tree grow and produce new seeds and fruit. Birds eat the energy-filled seeds and fruit from the trees and other plants. The birds use the energy from their food to grow, fly, and reproduce.

Millions of years ago, plants and animals used photons from the sun to store energy. Although the plants and animals died and were eventually buried, that energy remained within them. The dead organisms were squeezed and compressed over millions of years until they turned into petroleum. The petroleum was then refined into gasoline and pumped into your school bus.

Make Connections

When you read, try to think of a situation in your own life that is similar.

1. Tell about a time when you wanted to fit in with a group of people.

   _____

   _____

2. Read the story. Do you enjoy roller coasters? Explain.

   _____

   _____

3. What might have happened if the writer had "lost his lunch" on the very first ride?

   _____

   _____

4. What did the writer do that helped him to get along with Luis's friends?

   _____

   _____

Critical Thinking

How did making connections to your own life help you to understand the writer's emotions in this story?

_____

_____

_____

RIDES TO REMEMBER

My older brother Luis and his friends had hung out together for years. I've always wanted to be a part of their group. Now I was being given the chance to go with them to an amusement park, and I didn't want to blow it.

As we walked into the park, Luis fell back behind the group and called me over. He turned his back on his friends so that they couldn't see and took out his wallet to hand me two 20-dollar bills.

"Here, this is so you can buy your admission ticket," he said.

I felt really thankful that he didn't make a big deal of giving me money in front of his friends. After we moved through the gates, we ran all the way to "The Cliffhanger," a roller coaster famed for turning its passengers "green" with nausea. As I put one foot into the car, I hesitated, hoping I wouldn't be the one to lose his lunch. That would be so embarrassing! Luis was right behind me, laughing, as he pushed me the rest of the way into the car.

"You're not afraid are you?" he chuckled.

"No," I responded with more bravado than I felt.

Well, to make a long story short, I survived "The Cliffhanger" and 10 more roller coasters that day, even though each one seemed scarier than the last. As the day went on, I grew more confident and less afraid of sticking my foot in my mouth. I talked to Luis's friends and started feeling like I was part of the group.

Make Connections

When you read, try to think of a situation in your own life that is similar.

1. Tell about a time when you were "the new kid" in a neighborhood, club, team, school, or other situation.

   _____

   _____

   _____

2. Read the story. Is your personality like Connor's? Explain.

   _____

   _____

   _____

3. Think of a time when you wanted to make a good impression and felt like you failed. Describe it.

   _____

   _____

   _____

Critical Thinking

How did making connections to your own life help you to understand Connor's emotions in this story?

_____

_____

_____

The First Day at a New School

Connor was entering his first day in fifth grade, six weeks after school had started. His mom had gotten a new job in a different city. When he entered the new school, the halls were large and crowded with students walking to class. He was sure every kid was looking at him and some even smiled, but he didn't want to talk to anyone. He just wanted to be invisible.

After Connor met with the principal, Ms. Raphael, she escorted him to his classroom. The halls were empty now as everyone was in class, and he entered his classroom late. Mrs. Andrews, his teacher, assigned him his textbooks and piled them high in his arms. He could hear the other students whispering behind him and feel their eyes boring into his back. As Mrs. Andrews placed the last book on the stack, she told him to take the empty desk in the left row.

Connor walked down the narrow aisle, struggling under the weight of the heavy books. His arms were just about to give out when he reached his desk. When he started to set the books down, he heard Mrs. Andrews' firm voice, "Not that desk. The one in the next row."

Oh no! Connor had gotten his left and right mixed up again. He heard a few snickers from the other students, and his face grew warm and red. He pulled the pile of books back up to his chest and shuffled toward the next row. Reaching the correct desk, he set the books down and slid into the seat. Abruptly, the bell rang, signaling recess. Connor sighed with relief. He needed this time to regroup and start the day over.

Context Clues

If you come to a new word that you do not know, reread the sentence it is in. If that doesn't work, keep reading. Information after the word may give you a clue as to what it means.

Scan the text for boldface words. You will figure out the meanings for these words.

1. Read the text. What does the word *despised* mean? How do you know?

    _____

    _____

2. What does the word *astute* mean? How do you know?

    _____

    _____

3. What is an *eye opener*? How do you know?

    _____

    _____

Critical Thinking

How does using context clues help you to read more difficult texts?

_____

_____

_____

The Boy Who Hated Tests

Allen was a sixth grader who **despised** tests. He always felt sick on a test day. Even though he did pretty well in his daily work, when the teacher gave a test, he always scored poorly. He couldn't figure out why he bombed each exam until he talked about it with his mother. He had just brought his report card home. His mother looked it over, shook her head, and asked him why he got a D in math. "You know how to add, subtract, multiply, and divide. Why did you get such a low grade?"

Allen hung his head because he felt embarrassed about his lousy report card. He responded, "I do pretty well in math when we do our daily work, but I can't get it right when we take our weekly tests. The teacher says I have to do better on my tests if I want to raise my grades, but I hate tests!"

"I guess you're just like your dad and me," his mother told him. "We didn't do well on tests either. I was terrified of them, and your dad just couldn't figure them out. He had the same problem you have—he always did well until it came to a test."

"So that's it," Allen thought to himself, "Like father, like son—it just runs in the family. I may as well quit trying."

Fortunately, Allen had an **astute** teacher. She knew that Allen wasn't the only student in her class struggling with tests. So she introduced some games to teach them how to do better on tests. Before they even started the games, she taught them that tests were like sports, where you get a chance to show what you know. That idea was an **eye opener** for Allen, who had never thought of tests as games in which you competed against yourself and others as you do in computer games, basketball, or other sports. Also, his teacher emphasized that tests are a part of life. If you want to get a driver's license, you have to take a test. To go to college or to get a job, you have to take tests.

For the rest of the school year, Allen worked on learning test-taking techniques. Soon he learned to have fun competing with himself. Then he found himself not only doing well on tests but actually enjoying them! Since the scores on his tests were higher, his next report card showed improvement. He could hardly wait to show it to his mother. He handed it to her, saying, "Look, I got a B in math this time, and all my other grades are higher, too. I've learned that not doing well on tests doesn't have to run in the family, and I don't hate tests anymore!"

Context Clues

If you come to a new word that you do not know, reread the sentence it is in. If that doesn't work, keep reading. Information after the word may give you a clue as to what it means.

Scan the text for boldface words. You will figure out the meanings for these words.

1. Read the text. What is *agriculture*? How do you know?

   _____

   _____

2. What is another word for *appointed*? How do you know?

   _____

   _____

3. What does the term *bumper crop* mean? How do you know?

   _____

   _____

How does using context clues help you to understand this text?

   _____

   _____

   _____

George Washington Carver

George Washington Carver was born in 1864. He never knew his parents. His father died in a farming accident. Soon after that, slave raiders snatched his mother. All this occurred while George was still just an infant. A white couple named the Carvers raised him. They lived in Diamond Grove, Missouri.

By the time George was 12, he was excited about learning and knowledge. So he set out on foot to find a school that accepted blacks. His travels took him through Missouri and into Iowa and Kansas. While he went to school, he earned money by working as a farmhand, cook, and laundry helper.

In 1894, George graduated with honors from Iowa State College. He took a job there as the greenhouse director. During this time, he discovered a new kind of fungus that grows on the leaves of red and silver maple trees.

George Washington Carver

Many people began to hear about George's work in **agriculture**. Then a college named the Tuskegee Institute opened its doors to black students. George was **appointed** the head of its Department of Agriculture. Not only did George do research, but he was also in charge of teaching farmers. They had been planting cotton for years. But the soil lacked nutrients. To make matters worse, an insect called the boll weevil had destroyed thousands of acres of cotton. George told the farmers to plant peanuts instead of cotton.

The first season produced a **bumper crop** of peanuts. In fact, no one knew what to do with all of them! So, George went to work in his lab. He began analyzing the peanut. He found that he could extract a substance similar to cow's milk from peanuts and then make cheese from it. He figured out how to use peanut oil to make cooking oil, soap, and body oil. George discovered more than 300 products that could be made from peanuts! He also did extensive agricultural research on soybeans and yams.

George Washington Carver died on January 5, 1943. He is buried on the campus of the Tuskegee Institute.

Carver's lab at Tuskegee Institute

Visualize

When you visualize, you form mental images based on what you read. It is like making a movie in your mind. It's an important step to help you to comprehend what you read.

1. Read the first paragraph. Draw the picture that formed in your mind.

2. Read the second through fourth paragraphs. Draw the picture that formed in your mind.

3. Read the last paragraph. Draw the picture that formed in your mind.

Critical Thinking

How did picturing the story as it occurred help you to understand it?

_____

_____

_____

RUNNING LOBSTER TRAPS

Marcus liked helping his uncle run his lobster traps. It was fun riding out in the flatboat and pulling up the heavy box traps to see if there were lobsters inside. His uncle baited each trap with a morsel of food that a lobster would like. When a lobster came along, it would smell the food and push its way through the door at the end of the trap to reach it. Once the lobster went in, there was no way it could get out.

"How much do you know about our friend, the lobster?" his uncle shouted over the roar of the engine to Marcus one chilly morning. They were skimming across the water on their way home from the traps. His uncle was in a cheerful mood because they had made a particularly large catch.

"Not much, Uncle Carl, except that they are tasty," Marcus yelled back.

His uncle chuckled. "A mother lobster produces thousands of eggs. They are attached under the curve of her tail for protection for up to a year. Finally, she shakes them free, and they float on the water's surface. Most are eaten by birds and other sea animals."

Seeing the interest on Marcus's face, his uncle continued, "The few that survive grow and change shape until they are heavy enough to sink to the bottom. There they turn into tiny baby lobsters, only about one-third of an inch long (0.8 cm). When they become adults, they can grow to a length of two feet (0.6 m). That is when we catch them in our traps."

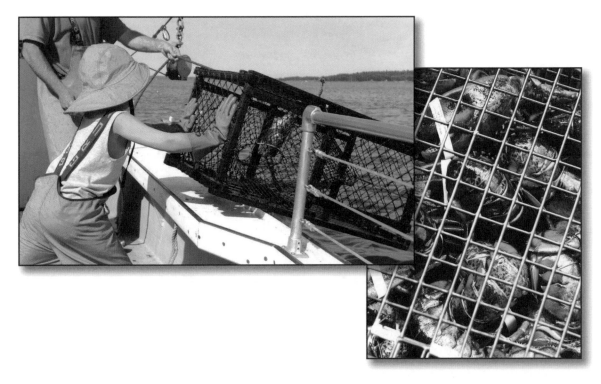

Visualize

When you visualize, you form mental images based on what you read. It is like making a movie in your mind. It's an important step to help you to comprehend what you read.

1. Read the first paragraph. Draw the picture that formed in your mind.

2. Read the second paragraph. Draw the picture that formed in your mind.

3. Read the third paragraph. Draw the picture that formed in your mind.

Critical Thinking

How did picturing the story as it occurred help you to understand it?

_____

_____

_____

Sofia's Quinceañera Gown

A quinceañera (keen-say-NYAIR-uh) is a celebration for a Latina girl turning 15. She is becoming a woman. Saturday is Sofia's quinceañera, and she can't wait to see her gown. Every day, she daydreams about posing for her photographs. She knows that her mom and dad want it to be a surprise. But she just can't resist the temptation to take a peek. So, as her parents watch television in the darkened living room, Sofia creeps towards the worn wooden staircase with its creaking steps. She slips off her flip-flops so as not to make that slapping noise. As she creeps upstairs, each step makes its own distinct sound. When she reaches the top, Sofia hears only the drone of the television and sees the flashing light from its images on the stairwell wall.

Sofia tiptoes down the dark upstairs hall. As she arrives at her parents' bedroom, she gently pushes the door open. The cat-like screech of the door hinges makes her jump! She holds her breath, but hears no movement downstairs. She quietly slips across the dark bedroom to the closet.

Sofia sees the large rectangular box on the closet's top shelf. She stretches her arms to reach around it, but the box slips from her grasp. She pushes herself up on her toes and stretches her arms as far as possible. Her hands grasp the sides of the box. She's got it! She slides the box soundlessly off the shelf and sets it on the floor. She eagerly lifts the lid, only to discover that the box is empty! All it contains is a folded sheet of paper with her name on it. The note reads, "Dear Sofia, You'll have to wait until Saturday. Love, Mom and Dad."

Story Elements

Every story has three elements: characters, a setting, and a plot. The plot is a problem and the way it gets resolved.

1. Before you read the story, glance at each paragraph. What are the names of the three characters?

   _____   _____   _____

2. Read the story. Describe this story's setting (where and when the story happens).

   _____

   _____

3. What is the conflict (or problem) in this story?

   _____

   _____

4. Is the conflict resolved by the end of the story? Explain.

   _____

   _____

   _____

Critical Thinking

Predict what will happen next in the story.

_____

_____

_____

Maritza's Dilemma

Maritza was the new girl in class. Her family had just moved to town, and she didn't know anyone, not even her neighbors! She was scared to death to go to her new school, but her mom and dad said she had to go anyway. Maritza had always been on the shy side. Making new friends was hard for her.

As she stood in front of the room being introduced by the teacher, a girl in the third row caught Maritza's eye. They smiled at each other, and Maritza relaxed a little bit. Maybe it wouldn't be so bad after all. She was happy when the teacher sat her right next to the girl who had smiled at her. She introduced herself as Chloe.

The two girls ate lunch together all week. Maritza was glad that Chloe was her new friend. Chloe even asked her to go shopping with her and her older sister, Cynthia. Maritza was delighted when her parents said that she could go.

On Saturday, the three girls went to the mall. They were standing at a rack of necklaces and bracelets when Maritza noticed that Cynthia had picked up something shiny. As Maritza watched, Cynthia quickly looked around and then slipped the shiny object into her pocket. Maritza couldn't believe her eyes! What was she supposed to do now?

Story Elements

Every story has three elements: characters, a setting, and a plot. The plot is a problem and the way it gets resolved.

1. Before you read the story, glance at each paragraph. What are the names of the two characters?

    _____   _____

2. Read the story. What is the setting for this story (time and place)?

    _____

3. What is the conflict (or problem) in this story?

    _____

    _____

4. Is the conflict resolved by the end of the story? Explain.

    _____

    _____

    _____

    _____

Critical Thinking

Predict what will happen next in the story.

_____

_____

_____

Sleepover at the Art Museum

Jennifer and Twila had been looking forward to this trip for months. Their Explorer Troop had arranged for a sleepover at the art museum. The day had gone well. The girls and their leader had learned a lot about the art that was housed here and the artists who had created it. But now it was late, and neither girl could sleep.

"Just lying here is silly," said Twila, "Let's go look at that painting again!"

Jennifer knew exactly which painting Twila meant. It was the one entitled "The Boy with the Haunting Eyes," and the title was apt. The boy stared out eerily, as if beckoning viewers to join him in the portrait. He seemed to want help with something, although there was no clue visible as to what. His expression gave Jennifer the creeps.

"They said not to leave the room after lights out unless we need to use the bathroom," Jennifer protested. "We'd need to get Ms. Lathy to go with us."

"I don't want to wake Ms. Lathy just because I'm an insomniac. I won't touch anything, but I need to see that picture again," Twila said sounding determined. She eased herself quietly out of her sleeping bag, turned on her flashlight, and padded softly across the room, careful not to disturb the slumbering girls. Then she slipped out the door and disappeared silently around a corner.

Jennifer hesitated. She had no desire to see that spooky picture again, and she didn't want to go with her friend. She knew they shouldn't leave the room. Still, when Twila hadn't returned after half an hour, Jennifer tiptoed out of the room.

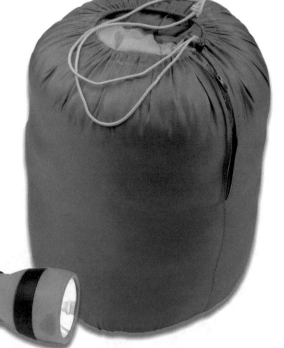

The painting was in a small alcove by itself, so Jennifer didn't see Twila until she almost tripped over her. Twila had fallen asleep. Jennifer shook her shoulder.

"I dreamed that I went into the painting and helped the boy!" Twila yawned.

"Tell me about it in the morning," Jennifer snapped. "Right now, let's get back to where we belong."

Plot

Every story has a plot. The plot has two parts. The first part is a problem. The second part is the way it gets resolved.

1. Read the text. Who is Raj?

   _____

2. Think about the events in the story. Fill in the problem and solution below.

Problem	Solution

3. What do you think will happen next?

   _____

Critical Thinking

It would be a plot twist if what Raj expects is not in the envelope. Why do writers have plot twists?

_____

_____

_____

The Auto Show

Ask Raj about a car—any car—and he can tell you anything you want to know: when it was built, what size engine it has, how the model has changed over the years. Cars are more than a hobby for Raj; they are his passion.

For years, Raj has dreamed about going to a big auto show. He'd be able to see all the newest models and even some concept cars that are years away from actual production. But the closest auto show is over four hours away, and it occurrs once a year. Raj's mom said it was too far for a one-day trip. Still, every year, Raj would cut out the advertisement from his favorite car magazine and leave it in an obvious place for his mom to see.

This year, the auto show is going to be the weekend after his birthday. Raj hopes this will be the year his mom will buy tickets and take him. However, on Raj's birthday, his mom handed him a huge box instead of the small ticket envelope for which he had hoped.

"Thanks, Mom," Raj said, disappointed at the sight of the box. He tried to smile and gave his mom a hug. When he opened the box, his face instantly lit up. Inside the gigantic, colorful box was a ticket envelope.

"Happy birthday, Raj!" his mom said with a smile.

Plot

Every story has a plot. The plot has two parts. The first part is a problem. The second part is the way it gets resolved.

1. One of the characters is not human. What is he and what can he do?

   _____

   _____

2. What is the problem in the story?

   _____

   _____

3. Is the problem solved by the end of the story? Explain.

   _____

   _____

   _____

Critical Thinking

Why do most stories have plots that are not solved quickly? Explain.

_____

_____

_____

An Important Race

Johan strapped into the cockpit on his Flight-Mec, Zoomer. This race wouldn't be like all the others. This time Johan and Zoomer would need to fly faster than they ever had before.

"Alright, Zoomer. Remember, we want to hit the flight deck running and jump as soon as we are clear!"

"Yes, Johan, I know what is expected. Need I remind you that I have performed this take-off procedure 150,863 times since my commissioning?" The 30-foot-tall flying robot sounded annoyed.

"Sorry. I'm just nervous and anxious! If we don't pass this assessment, the admiral might separate us," said Johan.

"They informed me that they were displeased when we created that sonic boom over the general's soufflé party."

"Um, yeah, that may not have been my best piloting decision. It was funny, though! All those fluffy eggs going flat did bring us some attention!" Johan stifled a chuckle and continued, "Anyway, they wanted to reassign you then and there. But I convinced them that no team in the whole Flight-Mec Fleet could beat us together!"

"Ah, they did not explain the circumstances to me during my flight preparation sequence. However, I might have guessed by using my probability protocols," replied the robot.

"Say, Zoomer, would you maybe do me a favor?" asked Johan.

"Would you like me to fly faster than all the other Flight-Mecs in the race?"

"If it isn't too much trouble," Johan smiled sheepishly.

"As you wish!" stated the giant robot as the official countdown began.

"3…2…1, Flight-Mecs LAUNCH!" boomed a voice.

Johan gasped and then grinned. Zoomer had launched perfectly and was already ahead of the other Flight-Mecs. He was indeed flying faster than he had ever done before! If they won, this team would be secure; they'd stay together for a long time to come.

Characters

When you read a story, it helps to think about each character. Try to picture him or her. What do you expect this person to say or do?

1. Read the story. Fill in the web below with words or phrases that describe Captain Butterbeard.

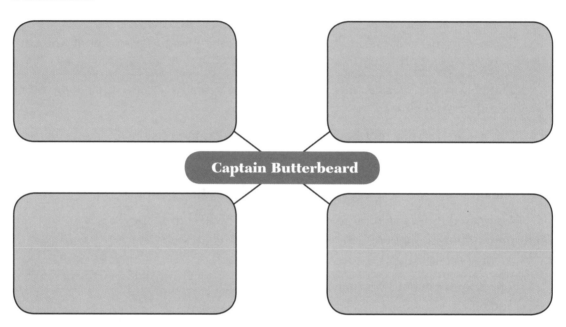

Captain Butterbeard

2. What can you tell about Captain Butterbeard's crew?

_____

_____

Critical Thinking

Think of a character you could add to this story. What would your character say or do?

_____

_____

_____

Captain Butterbeard Addresses His Crew

Captain Butterbeard looked suspiciously at his crew. Which one of them would betray him? He had selected each one of them. His ship had the foulest, most cutthroat crew of any pirate vessel in the Caribbean. While that made them very good at their jobs, it meant that not one of them could be trusted. The crew operated like a pack of wolves. The strongest one would lead until he was challenged successfully by an underling. Captain Butterbeard liked that about them.

"Ye scurvy sea dogs," Captain Butterbeard sneered. "Listen up! This here island is Tortuga and that there ship is the *Bonny Main*. Tonight, she plans to sail out of port laden with jewels, gold, and riches of all kinds. By tomorrow morning, her cargo will be stowed in our hold, and her crew will be secured in our brig, ready to ransom!"

The captain strutted confidently in front of the assembled crew. He knew that his biggest threat was not from the defenders on the *Bonny Main*. No, the risk was this crew would turn on him if they thought he showed even the slightest weakness. He must always project strength.

"I don't have to tell ye mates that we stand to make a small fortune on this haul, but we have to work together!" The captain stopped suddenly and stared directly into the eyes of a particularly cruel-looking crewman. "Every man here will pull his own weight, or he will be spending time in Davy Jones's locker!" The man shifted uncomfortably and looked away.

"Are ye with me, lads?" the captain finished.

The crew cheered enthusiastically, and then rushed off to follow his orders. Captain Butterbeard allowed himself a cautious smile. There would be no mutiny today!

Characters

When you read a story, it helps to think about each character. Try to picture him or her. What do you expect this person to say or do?

1. Read the title. Name one character that will be in the story.

   _____

2. Read the story. What can you tell about King Midas's personality?

   _____

   _____

3. Why does King Midas want to get rid of his "gift"?

   _____

   _____

4. What do you think King Midas learned from this experience?

   _____

   _____

Critical Thinking

Think about the characters other than King Midas. Why didn't the author include more information about them? Explain.

   _____

   _____

   _____

KING MIDAS'S GOLDEN TOUCH

Once there was a king named Midas who lived in what is now Turkey. King Midas was not a bad man, but he was greedy.

One day a man named Silenus got lost in Midas's kingdom. Midas offered to help Silenus and arranged to have the man taken home.

Silenus lived with the god Dionysus. Dionysus appeared before the king. "I would like to give you a reward for helping my friend," Dionysus said. "Ask me for anything and, if I can, I will grant you one wish."

Since Midas had just one wish, he wanted to be very careful about his choice. "I would like everything I touch to turn to gold," Midas said.

Dionysus looked at the king. "Are you certain that is what you desire?" he asked.

"Yes," replied Midas. "I am positive."

Dionysus granted the king's wish. Midas was excited and immediately put his new "gift" to the test. He touched a twig and a stone—they turned to solid gold. "I got my wish! Now I will be the richest man in the world!" King Midas cried as he ran into his palace and touched everything from floor to ceiling. Before he knew it, half the day had passed. When he realized how hungry he was, he went into his dining hall and sat at his golden table. Midas commanded his servants to bring him food. Hungrily, Midas grabbed a loaf of bread, but as soon as he did, it turned to solid gold. He grasped an apple, and the same thing happened. Midas told his servants to feed him, but as soon as any food touched his lips, it became hard, shiny metal. Now he realized his mistake.

"Dionysus!" he cried. "Help me! I will starve to death because of my wish!"

Dionysus took pity on him. "Not far from your palace is the River Pactolus," he told the king. "Go there and wash yourself in it, and your golden touch will be gone."

After King Midas did as he was told, he returned to normal. However, some of his golden touch remained in the River Pactolus. That is why to this day, if you look carefully, you can find gold dust there.

Title and Headings

Always read the title and headings before you read a text. They will tell you what the text will be about.

1. Read the title. Based on the title, what do you think the text will be about?

   _____

   _____

2. Read the text. Write one key piece of information for each heading.

   When and Where: _____

   _____

   Race Rules: _____

   _____

   What You Need: _____

   _____

   Who Can Enter? _____

   _____

Critical Thinking

How do the headings make this text easy to read quickly?

_____

_____

_____

Oysterville Crate Race

Can you walk on water?

Well, maybe you can by stepping on a row of wooden crates. The Oysterville Crate Race is a crazy way to take a swim, but a great way to have some fun!

When and Where

August 15 at Clear Lake Landing

Race Rules

For the race, 50 wooden crates are tied together between two piers. The crates float on the water, and racers must balance themselves as they run across the crates as fast as possible. Those who make it across all 50 crates must turn around and race back across them! The object is to cross as many times as possible without falling off.

What You Need

- sneakers
- a bathing suit
- good balance

Who Can Enter?

Boys and Girls:

- **Group 1:** ages 10 and under
- **Group 2:** ages 11–17

REGISTER BY August 1 at Oysterville Recreation

Prizes

- First place in each age group wins $25.
- Runner-up in each age group wins an oyster dinner.

Title and Headings

Always read the title and headings before you read a text. They will tell you what the text will be about.

1. Read the title and the headings. What do you think the text will be about?

   _____

2. Read the text. Write each heading and the purpose of that system.

   Heading: _____

   Purpose: _____

   _____

   Heading: _____

   Purpose: _____

   _____

3. How do the illustrations work with the headings to clarify the text?

   _____

   _____

   _____

Critical Thinking

Why did the writer use headings to divide this text into sections?

_____

_____

_____

An Amazing Machine

A machine has many parts that work together. In much the same way, a human body has systems that work together to keep a person alive. One system is not more important than another. All are necessary in order for the body to survive. Two body systems that work together are the circulatory system and the respiratory system.

The Human Circulatory System

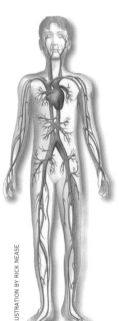

ILLUSTRATION BY RICK NEASE

The circulatory system moves blood throughout your body. Your cells need a constant supply of fresh blood. Blood has red blood cells, white blood cells, and platelets. The red blood cells carry oxygen from the lungs to the rest of your body. They also bring back carbon dioxide and waste. White blood cells destroy germs to keep your body healthy. Platelets stop bleeding by forming clots. In fact, without platelets, you could bleed to death from a small cut!

Your heart is a muscle and the pump of the circulatory system. Your heart is about the size of your fist. It pumps blood through blood vessels.

platelet

Actually, your heart has two pumps. The heart's left pump gets blood from your lungs. This blood has oxygen. Your heart pumps it to cells all over the body. Your heart's right pump gets the blood returning from the cells. This blood has carbon dioxide in it. The right pump moves this blood to your lungs. That's where carbon dioxide is removed from your blood and oxygen is added.

The Human Respiratory System

Your respiratory system gives your body oxygen and gets rid of carbon dioxide. When you inhale, your lungs get bigger, and oxygen rushes into them. When you exhale, your chest gets smaller, pushing carbon dioxide out. Air enters through your nose or mouth. Inside your nose are millions of tiny hairs. These hairs trap dust and dirt so that mostly clean air flows down your trachea to your lungs. Right above your lungs, the trachea splits into two tubes. One tube enters each lung.

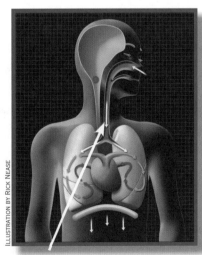

ILLUSTRATION BY RICK NEASE

trachea

Inside your lungs, these tubes branch into many smaller tubes. These smaller tubes have millions of air sacs. Carbon dioxide and oxygen get exchanged in these air sacs. Carbon dioxide leaves your blood and goes into the air sacs. Then oxygen moves through the air sacs into your blood. This oxygen-filled blood moves to your heart. The carbon dioxide leaves your lungs with the next exhale.

Typeface and Captions

A caption is a label given for an illustration. Words are set in a typeface. Typeface can be normal, boldface, or italics. When you see text set in one of these ways, it is a special typeface. It means the word is important.

1. Scan the text. What special typeface do you see in the text?

    _____

2. Write the words that are in the special typeface.

    _____   _____   _____

3. Read the text. Explain why those specific words are set in a special typeface.

    _____

    _____

4. Look at the photos and captions. How do the captions relate to the words in special typeface?

    _____

    _____

    _____

Critical Thinking

If you were unsure of the meaning of the words in the special typeface, how did the pictures help you?

_____

_____

_____

ZOOS: OLD AND NEW

The first zoo we know of was in Egypt around 1500 B.C. It belonged to Queen Hatshepsut. She received wild animals as gifts. They were given to her by people that her army had conquered.

Before modern zoos, some rich people had collections of animals called a **menagerie**. In most menageries, animals were kept in small, dirty cages. In modern zoos, animals are kept in areas that look more like natural habitats. This change took place slowly. For many years, the largest zoos kept animals in cages. Some zoos still keep animals caged. However, people often speak out against a zoo if its animals are kept in cages.

Long ago, the purpose of zoos was to let people see rare animals from distant places that most people could never visit. Today, there are additional reasons for zoos. Many animal species are **endangered**. This means that it is harder to find them in their native habitats. Some animals are no longer found in the wild at all. They exist only in **captivity**. Zoologists try to breed the captive animals. They want to return the species to its native habitat. Yet they are not always able to do this. Sometimes the habitat no longer exists due to changes in land use.

A cage in a menagerie from long ago

At one time, hunters captured and sold animals to zoos. This still occurs today. But now, zoos usually sell or trade their animals to other zoos. Many nations have passed laws against the capture of wild animals. Most zoo animals were born and raised in captivity.

People concerned with animal rights don't like zoos. Others feel that zoos care for and protect the animals. They say it is why many exotic species are still alive today.

An endangered white tiger in captivity

Typeface and Captions

A caption is a label given for an illustration. Words are set in a typeface. Typeface can be normal, boldface, or italics. When you see text set in one of these ways, it is a special typeface. It means the word is important.

1. Scan the text. What special typeface do you see in the text beneath the headings?

   _____

2. Read the text. Explain why those specific words are set in a special typeface.

   _____

3. Think about the examples given in the text. Then write a different real-life example for each of the following:

   absorption: _____

   _____

   refraction: _____

   _____

   reflection: _____

   _____

Critical Thinking

How do the captions relate to the words in special typeface?

_____

_____

_____

LIGHT

We can see because of light. Light waves bounce off objects and travel to our eyes. Our eyes and brains work together to translate that light into what we see. Light travels in waves much like water moves in waves. The amount of energy that a wave carries determines the color of the light. These waves differ from one another in length, rate, and size.

What happens when a light wave hits the atoms that make up all matter? Several things might happen:

- The light can be absorbed into the material.
- The light can change direction, or refract.
- Some of the light rays can reflect off the surface.

Absorption

Suppose a ray of light falls onto a piece of black cloth. The black cloth absorbs, or soaks up, almost all of the light rays. Such *absorption* means that almost no light is reflected from the cloth. If the surface upon which the light falls is perfectly black, there is no reflection at all. This means that the ray of light is completely absorbed. No matter what kind of surface light rays fall upon, some of the light gets absorbed.

Refraction

Light rays bend as they travel through the surface of transparent material such as the glass in a window. Transparent means that light can be seen through it and move through it. This bend in the light is called *refraction*. It occurs when light travels through different materials at different speeds.

reflection

refraction

Reflection

The return of a wave of energy after it strikes a surface is called *reflection*. Smooth and polished surfaces, such as mirrors and lakes, reflect more light than surfaces that are rough or bumpy.

When light reflects from a smooth surface, all of the light rays reflect in the same direction. A mirror is smooth, so you can see your image in it. When light reflects off a rough surface, the rays reflect in many directions. It is impossible to see your reflection in paper because the surface is rough.

Graphics

Always look at the pictures, maps, or diagrams before you read the text. They will give you clues as to what the text will be about.

1. Preview the text. Who is shown in the photograph?

   _____

2. What do you call the graphic that shows pictures and dates?

   _____

3. Read the text. Write the six terms that are in boldface print.

   _____   _____   _____

   _____   _____   _____

4. Look at the time line. Why were these terms boldfaced in the text?

   _____

   _____

   _____

Critical Thinking

How did the time line make the text more understandable? Explain.

_____

_____

_____

For the Record

Thomas Edison made the first sound recording in 1877. He sang, "Mary Had a Little Lamb." His recording machine was called the **phonograph**. It was hard to use. To record sound and play it back, someone had to turn a crank exactly 60 times a minute. Otherwise, the recording didn't sound right. At the time, people did not think his invention would be useful. They thought that the only way to hear music was to be in the same room with a musician.

The early recordings were cylinders covered with tinfoil. The phonograph had a needle that scratched the sound into the tinfoil. The recordings were unclear. In addition, they could only be played a few times before wearing out.

Ten years later, Emile Berliner made a better recording machine. It used a flat plastic disc. These "records" lasted much longer than the tinfoil cylinders. For the first time, people could buy music and play it many times.

Berliner's records held about two minutes of music. In 1948, Columbia Records introduced the **LP**, or long-playing record. One LP held up to 30 minutes of music per side. This meant that symphonies could be recorded. The LP changed music recording all over the world. It was invented at a good time. In the 1950s, popular music was taking off. Musicians wanted to make recordings, and people wanted to buy them. The LP let radio stations play different kinds of music. Once people heard the same song over and over, they wanted to buy it.

By 1962, people could also buy music on magnetic tape enclosed in a plastic case. These **cassette tapes** were cheaper and more portable than LPs. In 1979, Sony invented a portable machine that played cassettes. It let people listen to music anywhere.

Three years later, **compact discs (CDs)**, were created. They sounded better than any prior kind of recording. A CD could hold over an hour of music. CDs had replaced LPs by the 1990s.

Then, in 1998, a new invention hit the market: the **MP3 player**. It could store and play **digital audio** files. An MP3 player offers high-quality sound and is much smaller than a CD player.

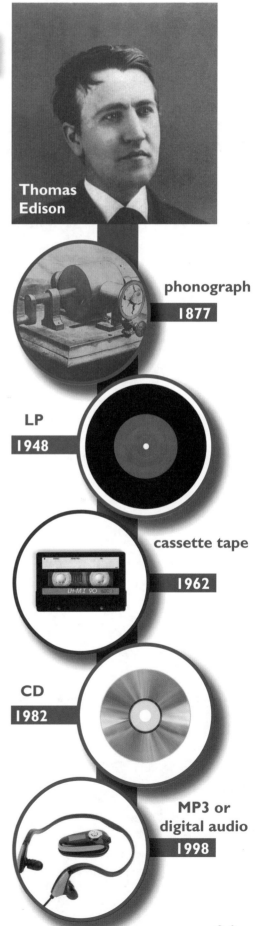

Thomas Edison

phonograph
1877

LP
1948

cassette tape
1962

CD
1982

MP3 or digital audio
1998

Graphics

Always look at the pictures, maps, or diagrams before you read the text. They will give you clues as to what the text will be about.

1. Preview the text. What is shown in the bottom photo?

    _____

    What is shown in the photo on the left?

    _____

2. What is shown in the diagram?

    _____

3. Read the text. Write the terms that are in italics.

    _____   _____   _____

4. Why are these words italicized?

    _____

    _____

Critical Thinking

How did the diagram help you to understand the text?

_____

_____

_____

Shaking and Quaking

You are going about your daily life. Suddenly, the ground shakes! Huge cracks open in the ground! What is happening? It's an earthquake. It can be caused in many ways: Earth's crust may slide, a volcano may become active, or humans may set off an explosion. The earthquakes that cause the most damage result from Earth's crust moving.

At first, the crust may bend due to pushing forces. When the pushing becomes too intense, the crust snaps and shifts. The place where this happens is called the *epicenter*. From there, waves of energy extend in all directions. They are kind of like the ripples you see when a stone is dropped in water. These are called *seismic waves*. The waves travel out from the center of the earthquake. Sometimes people can hear these waves because they make the planet ring like a bell. It is terrifying to hear this sound!

Crust movements can leave a crack, or fault, in the land. Geologists are the scientists who study Earth's surface. They know that earthquakes happen most often along fault lines. Earth's crust is weakest wherever there are faults. This means that earthquakes may happen repeatedly in those places.

When earthquakes happen under the ocean floor, they may cause huge sea waves called a *tsunami*. There was an earthquake off the shore of Alaska in 1964. Its giant waves caused more damage to some towns than the earthquake did. In 2004, another undersea earthquake caused a major tsunami that killed more than 300,000 people in Southeast Asia.

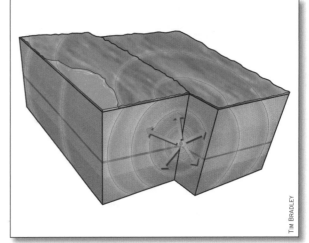

seismic waves

fault line

after an earthquake

Topic Sentences

A topic sentence is one that sums up what the paragraph is about. It is often the first sentence in a paragraph. Sometimes it is the last sentence in a paragraph. It can even be a sentence within the paragraph.

1. Read the text. Write the topic sentence used in the first paragraph.

   _____

   _____

2. Create a topic sentence for the second paragraph.

   _____

   _____

3. Write the topic sentence used in the third paragraph.

   _____

   _____

4. Answer the question posed in the last sentence of the text.

   _____

   _____

Critical Thinking

How can you use topic sentences the next time you read a nonfiction text?

_____

_____

_____

Earth's Cycling Seasons

Earth's spinning causes a cycle of changing seasons. It's a cycle because it repeats over and over without end. You know that there are four seasons each year: *spring, summer, autumn,* and *winter.* However, the seasons are not the same everywhere at the same time. For example, when it is winter in the Northern Hemisphere, it is summer in the Southern Hemisphere.

Earth orbits, or circles, the sun once each year. In other words, it makes one revolution. At the same time Earth is revolving around the sun, it is also spinning. Each day, Earth rotates, or turns, on its axis. This means that half of Earth is always experiencing daytime, and the other half is experiencing nighttime.

Earth's axis is not straight up and down; it tilts a little. So, Earth tilts a little, too. Since Earth is tilted, the sun's most direct rays strike Earth in different places as the planet revolves around the sun. When the sun is shining most directly on the Northern Hemisphere, it is summer. Now think: What season would it be in the Southern Hemisphere?

Topic Sentences

A topic sentence is one that sums up what the paragraph is about. It is often the first sentence in a paragraph. Sometimes it is the last sentence in a paragraph. It can even be a sentence within the paragraph.

1. Read the text. Write the topic sentence used in the first paragraph.

   _____

   _____

2. Write the topic sentence used in the second paragraph.

   _____

   _____

3. Write the topic sentence used in the third paragraph.

   _____

   _____

4. Write the topic sentence used in the fourth paragraph.

   _____

   _____

Critical Thinking

If you read this text in order to write a report about firefighters, how would making note of the topic sentences help you?

_____

_____

_____

FIREFIGHTERS

Firefighters are always busy. They can be called to a fire at any time of the day or night. They must be ready at all times in case of an emergency. That's why some firefighters live at the fire station part of the time. They have beds, a bathroom, and a kitchen there. They also have rooms for relaxing. If there is no fire, they get to sleep at night. When they are at the station, they check the equipment and the fire trucks. They inspect the hose nozzles to make sure they are working. They check the engine to be sure there is enough gas and oil, and make sure there is enough air in the tires.

Firefighters take turns doing the chores at the station. Sometimes they give tours of the fire station to students and other community groups. They show the equipment in the station and on the trucks.

Firefighters are busiest when they are called to an emergency. In addition to fires, they rush to help in many different emergencies. Sometimes firefighters are called to help people in medical emergencies. Sometimes they rescue people who are trapped in vehicles after a crash. Other times, they clear areas near fires or other disasters or pump out flooded basements. They help people after any kind of disaster: earthquakes, major storms, and terrorist attacks.

Firefighters keep busy even when there are no emergencies. They teach about fire safety in schools. They spend time practicing the best ways to put out various types of fires. They need to be ready no matter what happens. Firefighters inspect local businesses to make sure they are safe for both the workers and the customers.

© 2009 JUPITERIMAGES CORPORATION (/PHOTOS.COM)

Main Idea

The main idea is what a text is mostly about. In fiction, the idea is almost never stated in a sentence in the text. You have to read the whole thing and then think about what the main idea is.

1. Read the story. Who is the main character in the story?

   _____

2. What is he determined to do?

   _____

3. Write the main idea in the chart below. Then write six details that support the main idea.

Main Idea
Detail
Detail
Detail
Detail
Detail
Detail

Critical Thinking

Why doesn't the author ever tell you what type of creature Milo is?

_____

_____

_____

Milo the Victorious

Milo lounges in the patch of sunlight, his sleek tail flicking carelessly. He stretches, rolls, and then plops into a lazy crouch. Suddenly, his ears prick up. He sees a mortal enemy close by. The Pink Jingly Puff Ball must die!

Milo's body tenses. His eyes lock on his prey. His whiskers vibrate, ready to interpret even the slightest change in the air. The fully alert hunter hunches close to the wall and slowly begins his approach. He hides beside the cedar chest that stands at the end of the bed to await the perfect opportunity to strike.

"TING-ALING-ALING!" Horror fills Milo's heart as he realizes that the bell attached to his collar has sounded a warning. He freezes in place, quivering with excitement. The Puff Ball makes no sign that it has heard the bell. Milo feels triumphant. "I have you now!" he thinks gleefully.

Inch by inch, Milo creeps across the soft carpet. Suddenly, Milo springs full force on the Pink Jingly Puff Ball and grabs it firmly with his teeth. He gives a quick shake of his head and then waits expectantly. The puff ball shows no sign of life. Milo is victorious! Once again, the fierce hunter has protected his territory from the evil fluffy things of the world. Milo drops the vanquished foe and retreats to the sunny spot to clean himself, content in a job well done.

Main Idea

The main idea is what a text is mostly about. In nonfiction texts, the main idea may be stated in a sentence in the text.

1. Tell about a time when you saw or had a glowing light stick.

   _____

   _____

2. Read the text. The main idea is not stated, so you will need to combine ideas. Write the main idea below.

   _____

3. The details explain how the light stick works. Write the details below.

   _____

   _____

   _____

   _____

   _____

Critical Thinking

How does the main idea of a nonfiction text differ from the main idea of a fiction story?

_____

_____

_____

Light Sticks

You've seen light sticks. These days, they seem to be anywhere that there's a big crowd of people. You can buy them at fairs, circuses, amusement parks, and concerts. But what are light sticks and how do they work?

Most light comes from energy. Different kinds of energy make different kinds of light. The light that comes from a light bulb is different than the light that comes from a TV or a neon light. The light that comes from light sticks comes from a chemical reaction.

The outside of a light stick is made of plastic. It's filled with hydrogen peroxide, which is a common household chemical. Inside the light stick is a small glass tube filled with another chemical called *phenyl oxalate ester*. When you bend the light stick, the glass tube breaks. When the two chemicals mix, it causes a chemical reaction called *chemiluminescence*. This reaction makes the stick glow. Dyes within the stick make different-colored lights.

It's too bad that light sticks don't glow very long. If you put one in very hot water for about a minute, it will glow brighter for a while. But if you want to use your light stick the next day, put it in the freezer. Although that won't stop the light from fading, it will make it last quite a bit longer.

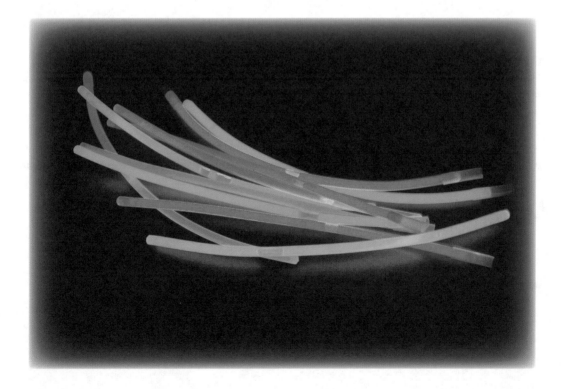

Details

As you read, ask yourself, "What is this text about?" That is the main idea. Then you can find the details that support the main idea.

1. Scan the text. What are the names of the two characters?

    _____   _____

2. Read the text. Write the main idea below.

    _____

    _____

3. The details of Max's dream made you form images in your mind. List the details that made Max's dream vivid.

    _____

    _____

    _____

    _____

    _____

Critical Thinking

Do you think it is easier to find the main idea and details in fiction or nonfiction? Explain.

_____

_____

_____

A Giant Red Ant

The day was hot, and the car was even hotter. Max was in the back seat with his older sister, Abby, as they rode in their parents' SUV. This was the summer trip Max had looked forward to for months, but he just couldn't stay awake. The slight vibration of the car and its gentle rocking motion were making him sleepy.

At the campsite, Max and Abby started to unpack the car. All of a sudden, Abby started screaming. Max turned to see that she was being carried into the woods by a giant red ant! Seeing a large tree next to where Abby was struggling with the ant, Max noticed a huge blister on the bark. The ant had pulled the struggling Abby near the tree just under the large blister. Max grabbed the camp ax and threw it at the tree with all his might. The ax blade slammed into the tree's blister and out gushed amber-colored liquid. It spewed all over the ant. As the ant struggled to free itself of the sticky goo, Max ran to his sister and grabbed her arms. He pulled hard, and she flew to one side. Yet no sooner had he freed her when the front legs of the ant grabbed his arms! The menacing pincers of its mouth snapped at his face.

Max tugged and pulled, screaming in terror. He could hear someone yelling in the distance. He opened his eyes and saw Abby's carrot-colored pigtails swaying beside her head, her glasses magnifying her eyes, and her hands wrapped around his wrists. She was shaking him. "Max! Max! Wake up! You're snoring again!"

Details

Skill Focus

As you read, ask yourself, "What is this text about?" That is the main idea. Then you can find the details that support the main idea.

1. Read the text. Write the main idea in the center of the graphic organizer below.

2. Write the most important details from the text in each of the boxes.

Detail
_____
_____
_____
_____

Main Idea

Detail
_____
_____
_____
_____

Detail
_____
_____
_____
_____

Detail
_____
_____
_____
_____

Critical Thinking

How do the details in nonfiction text differ from the details in fiction?

_____

_____

_____

Johnson Space Center

The United States is one of the leading countries for training astronauts. American astronauts begin their training at the Johnson Space Center in Houston, Texas. The center opened in 1961. Its name honors former President Lyndon B. Johnson, a Texas native. He was president in the 1960s, during a worldwide push to land people on the moon for the first time.

Inside the Johnson Space Center is the Mission Control Center. This is the huge room where people on Earth direct the space missions and talk to astronauts in space. They help the astronauts with the work they are doing. They help to solve problems that arise for the crew. Those in the Mission Control Center do all they can to keep the astronauts and their spacecraft safe.

Astronauts in training

Mission Control Center

What do astronauts do at the Johnson Space Center? They spend a lot of time in class, just like you do in school! They must learn the many skills they will need during their space travels.

Astronauts always travel into space in groups. They train with the people they will be with in space. It is important that astronauts work together as a team. Although each person has his or her own job, the crew will succeed—or fail—together.

Main Idea and Details

When you read, decide what the text is mostly about. That is the main idea. The main idea is supported by details. Some of the details are important. Others are not so important.

1. Read the text. Look for the main idea and details. Write the main idea of each paragraph.

Main Idea	Detail
Paragraph 1:	
Paragraph 2:	
Paragraph 3:	
Paragraph 4:	
Paragraph 5:	

2. Write one detail for the main idea of each paragraph.

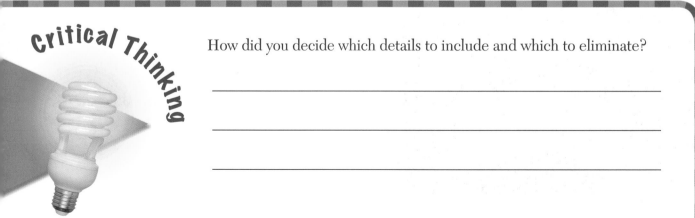

Critical Thinking

How did you decide which details to include and which to eliminate?

_____

_____

_____

Confucius, the Great Chinese Philosopher

In China long ago lived a man named Confucius. His teachings changed Chinese culture, and his influence continues today. Great thinkers called philosophers wondered about their laws and questioned, "Is this really right?" Confucius was one of these thinkers.

Confucius read many books that helped him think of ways in which his government could improve. He saw how the poor starved when the harvests failed. He watched the government abuse its power. Confucius wanted to help those in need, and he wanted to end wars. He devoted his life to this cause.

Confucius started a school and invited both nobles and peasants to learn. This was shocking. At that time, people believed that only nobles could be educated. Confucius knew that education could make people equal. His school was free. It had just one requirement: each student had to love learning.

Confucius taught his students that the government should help everyone have good lives. Rulers should earn their power through their concern for their people. He told his students to speak out against dishonest, corrupt rulers. It's not surprising that some rulers disliked him.

China would not be what it is today without Confucius's teachings. Other societies have followed his ideas as well. If Confucius were alive today, he would be amazed. He died thinking that he had not changed China. Yet he had changed the world.

Statue of Confucius

Chronological Order

Putting events in the order in which they occurred is called chronological order. It gives the events from start to finish. It is a good way to organize what happened in a text.

1. Read the text. Summarize in one sentence what occurred on the first day of the ancient Olympics.

   _____

   _____

2. Number these events in the order in which they occurred in the Greek Olympics from first to last (1–5).

   _____ 400-meter race

   _____ chariot races

   _____ presentation of olive wreaths

   _____ 800 meter bareback horse race

   _____ pentathlon

3. Reread the text. List three words the author used to show you the order of events.

   _____ _____ _____

Critical Thinking

Why do authors write events in chronological order?

   _____

   _____

   _____

THE ANCIENT OLYMPICS

In ancient times, male athletes arrived in Olympia, Greece, one month before the games. (Women did not compete in the ancient Olympics.) During this time, priests prepared them to become pure in thought and deed. The men spent time in physical training, too.

Day One: Worship marked the first day of the Olympic Games. Each athlete vowed to compete with true sportsmanship. Animals were sacrificed to the god Zeus near his grand temple.

Day Two: The second day began with chariot races. These races had two-wheeled carts drawn by four horses. Then came the 800-meter bareback horse race. This was followed by footraces, wrestling, boxing, and more horse racing.

Day Three: The third day was devoted to the pentathlon. Contestants competed in five different events in one day—a 200-meter run, long jump, discus throw, javelin toss, and wrestling.

Day Four: The final day of competition began with a 200-meter dash. The rest of the day was mainly devoted to wrestling and boxing. Wrestling contests took place in mud and dust. Dust made it easy to hold onto one's opponent. The mud made it more difficult. To win a wrestling match, an athlete pinned his opponent's shoulders to the ground three times. In boxing, athletes wore bronze caps to protect their heads from their opponent's fists, which were covered with hard leather gloves studded with metal.

Next came an event which combined wrestling, boxing, and judo. In this event, athletes could punch, kick, and even strangle their opponents until they surrendered! Then, to complete the Olympic Games, men wearing full armor ran a 400-meter race.

Day Five: Awards were given. This day began with more sacrifices to Zeus. The winners' names were read aloud before the altar of Zeus. The victors received a wreath of olive leaves to wear on their heads. They won prizes such as olive oil, fine horses, and privileges (such as not having to pay taxes or being excused from military service). These men returned to their city-states as honored heroes.

Chronological Order

Putting events in the order in which they occurred is called chronological order. It gives the events from start to finish. It is a good way to organize what happened in a text.

1. Read the text. Number the sentences in the correct order from first to last (1–4).

   _____ Shadwell is replaced by Monticello.

   _____ Jefferson takes a stand against British control of the colonies.

   _____ Jefferson is elected as the third U.S. president.

   _____ Jefferson learns to read five different languages.

2. On the time line below, write what event occurred in Thomas Jefferson's life for each date. Not all the dates are given in the text so you must figure some of them out for yourself.

1743	_____
1760	_____
1770	_____
1776	_____
1801	_____

Critical Thinking

If you were to write about your life, what events would you include in chronological order? Explain.

_____

_____

_____

THOMAS JEFFERSON

A lucky little boy named Thomas Jefferson was born in Virginia on April 13, 1743. Jefferson was lucky because his family lived on a beautiful plantation called Shadwell. There was lots of land for him to explore. He rode horses and learned to hunt. He loved the outdoors.

Jefferson was also lucky because he had an excellent mind. He loved to learn. His family hired tutors for him. He read books each day. He could read in five languages!

Jefferson grew up to be tall and thin with red hair and freckles. He was shy and did not talk very often. When he was 17, he went to the College of William and Mary. During his two years there, Jefferson worked very hard. Most days, he studied for 14 hours. He kept notebooks where he wrote down his thoughts about all the things he learned.

Thomas Jefferson

After college, Jefferson studied law for five years. Then he became a lawyer. He traveled all over Virginia. He liked meeting different kinds of people. Jefferson had many interests besides the law. In fact, it was hard to find a subject that did not interest him. He collected books on all sorts of subjects.

In 1770, Shadwell burned to the ground. Jefferson had a new mansion built on the plantation and named it Monticello.

By this time, many American colonists were unhappy with Great Britain. They did not like being told what to do by a king who lived so far away. Jefferson thought that the people should be able to make their own laws. He wrote about this in booklets and newspaper articles. Later, he was the main author of the Declaration of Independence, and in 1801, he became the third president of the United States.

Jefferson Memorial

Logical Order

Logical order is putting information in an order that makes sense. For example, you would tell what you plan to do on a weekend in the order in which you think you will do it.

1. Read the text. Imagine that you will tell someone how to create a compost pile. Write the steps in the correct order in the graphic organizer below.

    > **Step 1**

    > **Step 2**

    > **Step 3**

2. Use the words *first*, *then*, *next*, and *last* to write a short paragraph telling how to make a compost pile and use the compost.

    _____

    _____

    _____

    _____

Critical Thinking

Why is it a good idea to create a compost pile?

_____

_____

_____

Help Nature to Recycle

Stop! Don't throw dead leaves, grass clippings, and fruit and vegetable peels in the trash. Put them to good use in a compost pile.

Composting is nature's recycling method. It is a simple way to reuse plant waste. Composting breaks down plant materials into soil with lots of minerals. Adding composted soil to a garden helps to grow stronger, healthier plants.

Making your own compost is easy. First, gather "food" for bacteria and fungi. Then, let them do their job. Just follow these easy steps:

1. Choose a spot in your yard to place a bin. You can buy one or make one from wire or wood. It doesn't require a lid. That way, when it rains, the pile will get wet. Water helps the materials decay.

2. Throw kitchen scraps into the pile—things like tea bags, orange rinds, and potato peels. When you cut your grass, add the clippings to the pile. As a general rule, you can add any brown or green plant matter. Although you can put in eggshells, never add animal droppings, cheese, or pieces of meat or fat. These things take a long time to break down.

3. About twice a month, you must turn the pile to allow the rotting materials to get more air. Use a shovel to dig it up a bit. The bacteria and fungi that break down compost need air to live.

After just one year, the compost pile will look like soil. This material is called *humus*. Humus contains many other minerals that plants need. Spread the humus on your garden and watch your plants grow. After they die, add them to the compost pile. Then you can recycle those minerals again!

Logical Order

Logical order is putting information in an order that makes sense. For example, you would tell what you plan to do on a weekend in the order in which you think you will do it.

1. Read the text. Why is Aunt Emilia skeptical about the project in the beginning?

   _____

   _____

2. Look at the Things You Need list. How many foam cups are required for the project?

   _____

3. Read the instructions. Where can you get vermiculite?

   _____

4. How many steps will it take to get the project started?

   _____

5. After which step must the most time pass?

   _____

Critical Thinking

How did Aunt Emilia's ideas about hydroponics change?

_____

_____

_____

HYDROPONICS

"Raising plants without dirt? What a bunch of baloney. I've never heard of such nonsense!" exclaimed my Aunt Emilia. "A garden needs lots of good, fertile soil."

"But it's true," I insisted. "We learned all about it today in class. It's called *hydroponics*, and it's the cultivation of plants in water instead of soil. People have actually been doing it successfully for thousands of years. Look, here is a list of the things needed and how to do it." I handed her the instructions my teacher had distributed.

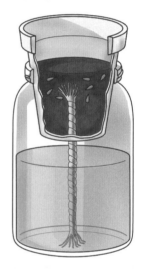

Things You Need
- wide mouth jar—a pint or quart size works nicely
- one foam cup that fits tightly in the neck of the jar
- piece of cotton rope long enough to reach from the bottom of the jar up into the foam cup
- seeds—green beans, lettuce, radishes, or peas work best
- vermiculite, which is a mixture of aluminum, magnesium, and iron, used instead of dirt as a medium for growing plants; available at garden shops
- hydroponic fertilizer—available at garden shops

Instructions
1. Fray both ends of the rope. This will be your wick.
2. Put the rope through the bottom of the cup and hold it there while you fill the cup with vermiculite.
3. Make plant nutrient by mixing hydroponic fertilizer in water.
4. Fill the jar so that the plant nutrient water does not touch the bottom of the cup.
5. Put the foam cup in the jar so the wick hangs down in the plant nutrient water.
6. Plant your seeds in the vermiculite (but not too deep).
7. Place your pot where it will get plenty of sunlight.

hydroponic garden

"I'm thinking of doing it for my science project this year. Will you help me, Aunt Emilia? You are always so good at growing things!"

A few days later, when the plants had sprouted, Aunt Emilia announced that she enjoyed hydroponics. She told me, "You know, the only thing wrong with hydroponic gardening is your hands don't get dirty!"

Fact and Opinion

A fact is something that can be proven. An opinion is what someone thinks. Today is rainy is a fact. You can prove it by looking outside. Rainy days are wonderful is an opinion. Not everyone would agree!

1. Read the text. Will every student be as delighted with the changes in school lunches as Amy Woods appears to be? Explain.

   _____

   _____

2. Read each statement. Write *F* for Fact or *O* for Opinion.

   _____ The school administration decided to change the school lunch program.

   _____ You'll be proud to eat healthy!

   _____ Vegetarian entrees will be available.

   _____ On Monday, our school lunch program will change.

   _____ Most of you will love these changes right away.

3. "Obesity is a big problem on our campus." Can you tell if this quote is a fact or an opinion? Explain.

   _____

   _____

Critical Thinking

Is Amy an objective reporter, or did she put some of her own opinions into the newscast? Explain.

_____

_____

_____

Change Comes to School Lunches

Principal: Good morning, students. Here's the morning news from sixth-grade reporter Amy Woods.

Amy: Great news! The school administration has decided to change our school lunch program. As of this Friday, say good-bye to the terrible chicken nuggets and awful nachos that we usually have. On Monday, our lunch program becomes healthy. We'll have an organic salad bar with plenty of fresh fruits and vegetables. We'll have delicious grilled chicken sandwiches, fish tacos, and whole-wheat pasta. There will be plenty of vegetarian entrees, too, like tofu burgers.

There will be no more greasy potato chips or fattening ice cream. Instead, we'll have baked crisps and frozen yogurt. The only drinks will be water, fruit juice, and skim milk. Most of you will love these changes right away. For others, it will take some time to get used to eating healthy.

Obesity is a big problem on our campus, and our lunch program has been partly to blame. These changes are long overdue.

Try all the great new foods offered for lunch. You'll be proud to eat healthy!

Fact and Opinion

A fact is something that can be proven. An opinion is what someone thinks. Today is rainy is a fact. You can prove it by looking outside. Rainy days are wonderful is an opinion. Not everyone would agree!

1. Read the text. Write one fact about Picasso from the second paragraph.

   _____

   _____

2. Besides painting, what other mediums did Picasso use?

   _____

   _____

3. Read each statement. Write *F* for Fact or *O* for Opinion.

   _____ These are the saddest paintings ever created.

   _____ His best paintings were his abstracts.

   _____ Picasso used geometric shapes to represent people and objects.

   _____ The artwork he created during his blue period was far superior.

   _____ Pablo Picasso is one of the best-known artists of the 20th century.

Critical Thinking

Why is Picasso best known for creating cubism?

_____

_____

_____

Pablo Picasso

Pablo Picasso is one of the best-known artists of the 20th century. He has influenced every artist who came after him.

Picasso was born in 1881 in Malaga, Spain. Even at a young age, his artistic talent was recognized as extraordinary by all who knew him. Picasso was admitted to the Royal Academy of Art in Barcelona, Spain, when he was just 15. At age 19, he moved to France.

Picasso's paintings are often grouped by his different styles. In his "blue period," his paintings showed images of poor people and were painted in tones of blue. These are the saddest paintings ever created. During his "rose period," Picasso used lighter colors and painted scenes from circus life. Although these masterpieces are more upbeat, the artwork he created during his blue period was far superior.

Picasso is best known for his creation of an art style called *cubism*. He used geometric shapes like cubes and cones to represent people and objects. When you first see these paintings, it's hard to figure out what you're looking at. As you look more closely, you can see the unique vision that went into creating them. His best paintings were his abstracts, in which nothing looks like what it's supposed to be.

Later, Picasso tried working in other mediums, including ceramics and sculpture. In fact, you may have tried one of his other styles, in which he attached bits of paper and other scraps to a canvas. It's called *collage*.

Early paintings by Pablo Picasso at the Picasso Museum

Proposition and Support

A proposition is a writer's opinion. The writer wants the reader to agree. So the writer gives support (reasons and information) to get the reader to share the same opinion. Often the writer states a problem and offers solutions.

1. Read the title. What do you think the proposition will be?

   _____

2. Read the text. What is the problem identified by the writer?

   _____

3. Name two of the solutions the writer suggests to solve the problem.

   _____

   _____

4. List the phrases from the text that let you know it addresses a problem and solution.

   _____

   _____

   _____

   _____

Critical Thinking

What do you think is the most realistic solution to the problem? Explain.

_____

_____

_____

School Garbage

At the end of the day, have you ever noticed the overflowing trash cans in our school? If you looked through the trash cans, you might find plastic, foam, glass bottles, food waste, paper, and much more. Most of these items should be recycled, or we could avoid their use altogether. We are generating way too much garbage in our school.

One solution to the problem would be to set up a recycling program at our school. Next to the trash cans, we could have recycling bins for paper, glass, and plastic. In every classroom, there could be recycling bins for paper. Students could be in charge of running the recycling program once it got off its feet.

Another solution that I propose is for students and teachers to make an effort to bring less garbage in their lunches. Instead of a paper lunch bag, bring a cloth reusable bag or a lunch box. Use reusable plastic containers instead of plastic baggies. Use a cloth napkin instead of a paper one. As for plastic cutlery, we should use real forks, knives, and spoons and put them through the dishwasher. And how about all the juice boxes and soda cans we bring? Instead, we could bring our drinks in reusable thermoses.

If all of these suggestions were implemented, we would have a lot less garbage at our school.

Proposition and Support

A proposition is a writer's opinion. The writer wants the reader to agree. So the writer gives support (reasons and information) to get the reader to share the same opinion. Often the writer states a problem and offers solutions.

1. Read the title and look at the photo. What do you think the author's proposition will be?

   _____

   _____

2. Read the text. Why has global warming caused problems for reindeer and caribou?

   _____

   _____

   _____

3. What does the writer want you to do as a result of reading this text?

   _____

   _____

Critical Thinking

Was the writer successful in persuading you to take steps to reduce global warming? Explain.

_____

_____

_____

Fighting for Survival

When we think of reindeer, the first thing that comes to mind is Santa Claus. But most reindeer are not being taken care of by a jolly old man. They are wild animals facing a serious threat to their survival. A study by the University of Alberta in Canada found that the number of reindeer and caribou (KARE-uh-boo) has dropped by about 60 percent over the past 30 years.

Reindeer and caribou are closely related deer species. They live in some of the coldest parts of the world. Caribou live in North America, while reindeer roam Scandinavia and Siberia.

Logging, mining, and the building of oil and gas pipelines have destroyed their natural habitats. Even so, experts say global warming is the biggest factor for the decrease in reindeer and caribou populations. Many factors, including the burning of coal, gas, and oil, have caused temperatures on Earth to rise. Reindeer and caribou have always lived in very cold, snowy areas. Now that Earth is warming, it is common to see freezing rain in these parts of the world. That means that the animals' food is often covered with ice. Reindeer and caribou eat a fungus on the ground called lichen (LIKE-en). When it's covered with ice, the deer can't smell it or, if they do find it, they struggle to grasp it with their teeth. Without adequate food, they will starve. If global warming continues, many more species will be in trouble.

You can help fight global warming by using less energy. Turn off the lights and TV when you leave a room. Take shorter showers. Turn down the heat in the winter and allow higher temperatures when using air conditioning.

Author's Purpose

When you read, ask yourself why the author wrote the text. Read carefully to determine the author's view about the topic.

1. Read the text. Why did the author write this email?

    _____

    _____

    _____

2. What does Eddie hope will be the result of this email?

    _____

    _____

    _____

3. Why did Eddie choose to write an email rather than talk to Jared?

    _____

    _____

    _____

Critical Thinking

How do you think Jared will respond to this email?

_____

_____

_____

I'm Sorry

To: jared@email.com

From: eddie@email.com

Subject: I'm sorry

Hey Jared,

I want to apologize to you for what happened yesterday. I didn't get a chance to tell you the whole story. First of all, I only meant to borrow your bicycle for about 15 minutes. The thing is, I wanted to go to Sound Town to buy a new CD. My mom couldn't take me, and my bike is broken. I saw your bike on your front lawn, but I didn't see you around. The only reason I didn't ring your doorbell was that I didn't want to bother anybody. Also, I didn't think you'd miss the bike for such a short time. And I thought that somehow if you did notice it was gone, you'd know I took it. I don't know why I thought that.

I should have left a note, but I didn't have any paper handy. Anyway, I was going to bring your bike back as soon as I bought the CD. The problem was, I ran into Jimmy and some other guys in Sound Town. They wanted to bike over to the mall to get a slice of pizza, and I was hungry.

When the police stopped me at the mall, I was shocked. They said I had stolen your bike. They took the bike and put me in the police car. I told them I only borrowed the bike, but they didn't listen. They just said they were going to arrest me and tell my parents. I was really upset and scared. That's why when they drove me to your house to make sure it was your bike, I freaked out. I yelled at you for calling the police. That was totally wrong. I should have apologized to you right then. Why wouldn't you think someone had stolen your bike? You had no way of knowing I had borrowed it.

I acted even worse after you and your mom told the police to let me go. I should have thanked you for keeping me out of trouble. But I ran home because I was so scared by what had happened.

Now I realize I was to blame right from the start. I should have asked you if I could borrow the bike. I had no right to just take it. Anyway, I'm really sorry. I hope you will forgive me for doing such a dumb thing. I want to stay friends.

Eddie

Send

Author's Purpose

When you read, ask yourself why the author wrote the text. Read carefully to determine the author's view about the topic.

1. Read the text. Why did the author write this text?

   _____

   _____

   _____

2. How does the author feel about visiting Saturn? How do you know?

   _____

   _____

   _____

3. Why did the author use this format to tell the reader about Saturn?

   _____

   _____

   _____

Critical Thinking

Where would you most likely read a text like this? Explain.

_____

_____

_____

A VISIT TO SATURN

Mom and Dad asked me what I would like to do for summer vacation this summer. I think they were hoping to go camping in the mountains. Everybody does that! I decided that I would like to go a little farther away than that. I dreamed about going camping—on Saturn. To find out what I would need to bring with me, I went to the library and read about Saturn.

Saturn is very far away, and it would take a long time to get there. It is over 900 million miles from Earth!

I would have to wear a special space suit to land on Saturn. It is a huge planet, and its gravity would be much stronger than Earth's. A space suit would have to be able to stand up under the crushing gravity.

Saturn's atmosphere is mostly hydrogen gas. We would probably be surrounded by clouds of ammonia ice crystals blown around in the strong winds that circle Saturn.

The rings around Saturn would be amazing to see up close. They are actually not solid rings. The rings are made of tumbling chunks of rock and glittering ice, through which it would be tricky to fly.

I told Mom and Dad my idea about camping on Saturn. Surprisingly, they liked the idea, too. Unfortunately, we don't own a spaceship, so I guess the only way I'll get to see Saturn close up is in the pages of a book!

Compare and Contrast

When you compare, you focus on how things are the same or similar. When you contrast, you focus on how things are different.

1. As you read the text, think about how dance and softball are alike for Jasmine. Notice how they are different. Read the story. Then fill in the chart below with Jasmine's ideas about each activity.

Softball Facts	Dance Facts

2. What are your passions?

_____

3. If you had to choose just one, which would it be and why?

_____

_____

Critical Thinking

Look at the chart. Predict Jasmine's final choice from what you listed in the chart above.

_____

_____

_____

A Difficult Choice

Ever since she was a toddler, Jasmine loved to dance. She was always twirling and leaping around the house. Jasmine's mom noticed her talent and enrolled her in ballet classes when she was five. As she got older, Jasmine tried different types of dance: jazz, tap, hip-hop, and salsa. She loved them all, and her teacher said she was improving all the time.

Dancing wasn't the only thing that Jasmine loved. She was a pitcher for her softball team, and her best friend, Isabella, was catcher. Jasmine had been playing for several seasons and always looked forward to getting out on the field.

She had always been able to fit both activities into her schedule. But this spring, it would be different. Her dance class was entering competitions on Saturdays, the same day of the week as her softball games. Also, Jasmine's mom worried that she wouldn't have enough time for studying.

"You'll have to make a decision," her mom said. "Dancing or softball."

Jasmine couldn't imagine giving up either, so she decided to make a list of all the facts for each sport. Both dancing and softball were great exercise, although she felt dancing made her not only stronger, but also more flexible. While she had friends in her dance class, her best friend was on her softball team. Her dance team spent most of the time practicing and not much time performing. In softball, time was evenly split between practices and games. And there was nothing more fun than the roar of the crowd when someone got a homerun.

But when it came time to make a final choice, Jasmine threw out the list. She had to follow her heart. When she tried to imagine life without one of her passions, she knew the one she couldn't live without was dance.

Compare and Contrast

When you compare, you focus on how things are the same or similar. When you contrast, you focus on how things are different.

1. Read the text. Fill in the Venn diagram to tell the similarities and differences between the African savanna and the Sahara Desert.

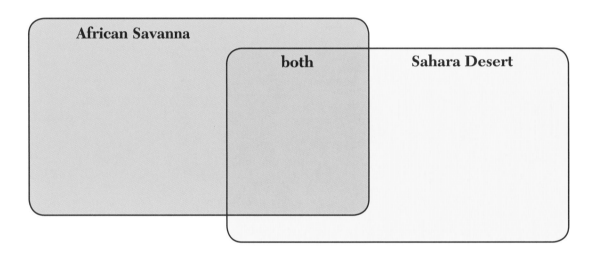

African Savanna   **both**   **Sahara Desert**

2. What is the name of the most well-known grassland in Africa? _____

3. Explain the difference between the climates of the savanna and the Sahara.

   _____

   _____

Critical Thinking

Which ecosystem would you rather visit? Explain.

_____

_____

_____

African Ecosystems

The Savanna

Tall, thin grasses rustle and sway in the breeze. A herd of zebras runs past in graceful bounds. In the distance, an elephant's trumpet sounds. Lions and leopards stalk their prey. This is the world of the grasslands. One of the most beautiful and famous of the grassland areas is the Serengeti Plain. It is found in Tanzania, a country in eastern Africa.

The Serengeti is usually warm and dry. However, it does rain from March to May and a little during October and November. In the Serengeti, it is coldest from June to October.

The most important feature of grasslands is that they are covered with grass all year long. Grasslands also have trees and bushes, but they are scattered and spread apart. Types of trees that grow in the grasslands include palm, pine, and acacia.

The grasses, bushes, and trees are important for animals. Many of them eat these plants for food. Water is also important for all living things. Because of wet and dry seasons and baking from the sun, the soil in some areas of the grasslands hardens. When it rains, the water does not soak into the ground. Instead, it may pool up for many months, providing water for the animals.

zebras in the African grasslands

The Sahara Desert

The Sahara is the largest hot desert in the world. It covers most of North Africa. More than 25 percent of the Sahara is covered by sheets of sand and sand dunes. The rest is made up of mountains, stony steppes, and oases. Sand dunes are hills or ridges of sand piled up by the wind. Some sand dunes and ridges get to be 500 to 1,000 feet (152.5 to 304.8 m) high!

The Sahara is very dry, but there is an annual rainfall in most regions. Half of the Sahara receives less than an inch (2.5 cm) of rain a year. The rest of it receives up to 3.9 inches (9.9 cm) a year. The northern and southern parts of the Sahara have slightly different climates. Summers are especially hot in the desert. The highest temperature ever recorded was 136°F (57.7°C) in Libya. Yet at night, the temperature can drop to freezing!

Animal life in the Sahara mainly includes gazelles, antelopes, jackals, foxes, badgers, and hyenas. Near the oases and along the rivers, plant life includes grasses, shrubs, and trees.

sand dunes in the Sahara

Classify

Sometimes when you read, you find groups that go together. For example, you can group shapes, colors, or animals.

1. Read the text. Then identify which foods below are sweet, sour, salty, and bitter. Write each one in the correct column in the chart below.

cookies	lemons	pretzels	coffee beans
potato chips	crackers	grapefruit	dill pickles
limes	cupcake	bananas	unsweetened cocoa

Sweet	Sour	Salty	Bitter

2. What happens to your sense of taste when you have a bad cold?

_____

_____

Which taste does your tongue like the best? Explain.

_____

_____

_____

Taste

What exactly does your tongue do when you take a bite of food? It goes through a lot of work to tell you if you like the flavor or not!

The taste buds on your tongue are in groups called *papillae*. These groups are connected to nerves. When you eat something, the taste buds give the nerves information. The nerves send messages to your brain about what you have eaten. Then your brain tells you what the taste is. This all happens lightning fast.

The four different tastes are sour, salty, sweet, and bitter. But would you believe that your taste buds don't react differently to the four tastes? That's why some scientists think that we learn to taste sour, salty, sweet, and bitter.

Did you know that you need your nose in order to taste? You must be able to smell to tell the flavor of a food. So, if you don't like how something tastes, hold your nose while you eat. That might help you not taste it.

Classify

Sometimes when you read, you find groups that go together. For example, you can group shapes, colors, or animals.

1. Read the text. On the chart below, classify the items read or checked out from the library by each boy.

Boy	Materials Used at the Library	Materials Checked Out to Take Home
Andy		
Kyle		
Colby		

2. Which boy seems to prefer fiction over nonfiction? _____

   How can you tell?_____

   _____

Critical Thinking

What materials do you most enjoy checking out from the library and why?

_____

_____

_____

At the Library

Andy, Kyle, and Colby met at the public library each Saturday afternoon. They had to return the materials they'd checked out and get some new ones. They dropped their things off at the counter and sat down at the computer catalogs.

Andy didn't need much time. All he ever read about was baseball. The library had everything he could ever want to know about baseball. This made Andy a big fan of the library. He disappeared into the maze of shelves to get his books.

Colby and Kyle went to find their own materials. Colby picked out a thick book about spiders and another one about snakes. Kyle met him in the aisle. He'd already found three spy novels and two graphic novels (also about spies). He found a seat and started reading the comics.

Colby picked up a magazine with a big picture of a shark on the cover. He sat down beside Kyle and read about sharks. After a while, the librarian announced that the library was closing soon.

As they went to check out, Colby traded his magazine for a film about sharks. Kyle found two movies that he wanted to see, both with spies and long car chases. The boys checked out their items at the desk. But where was Andy? They looked around but didn't see him.

Finally, just as the library was closing, Andy met his friends at the front desk. He had been reading a baseball magazine. Andy checked out two books and a movie about—what else?—baseball!

Cause and Effect

Skill Focus

A cause makes something happen. The effect is what happens. When you read, notice cause and effect relationships. This will help you to understand how and why things occur.

1. Read the text. Write the cause or effect for each event below.

Cause: The cat's movements are very quiet.
Effect:
Cause:
Effect: The mice want to put a bell around the cat's neck.
Cause:
Effect: No mouse volunteers to put the bell around the cat's neck.

2. Has the problem been solved by the end of the story?

_____

_____

Critical Thinking

Why did the old mouse shake his head sadly?

_____

_____

_____

Belling the Cat

The mice could stand it no longer. From everywhere in the house, they gathered in the Great Hall of Discussion, which was really just the old broom closet in the basement by the water heater. They needed to decide what to do about their great enemy, the cat.

"That cat is so dangerous; she'll destroy hundreds of us!" shouted one mouse angrily.

"Thousands!" agreed another.

"Order! Order!" demanded a fat mouse with a long tail. He drummed his foot on the water heater to get everyone's attention. When all the mice had settled down, the fat mouse said, "We are here to discuss what to do about the cat."

"She must be stopped!" squeaked a frightened voice. It came from a young mouse who had barely escaped the cat's claws—claws that were as sharp as fishhooks.

"I agree," said the fat mouse. "We need protection from her. But what can we do?"

"I know!" cried one of the mice. He was thin and nervous. He had not dared to steal food from the kitchen for three weeks. "The cat is deadly because we can't hear her coming. We must be able to hear her!" All the mice nodded in agreement.

"But how? What can we do to make the cat louder?" questioned the fat mouse.

"Tie a bell around her neck!" replied the thin mouse excitedly. "If she has a bell on a collar around her neck, every time she tries to sneak up on us, we'll hear it ring!"

The mice looked at each other and cheered. This was the best idea anyone had ever had for dealing with the cat. A bell! It was perfect! They jumped up and down. The only mouse who wasn't overjoyed was an old mouse. He shook his head sadly.

"All right, it's settled," shouted the fat mouse. "We'll tie a bell around the cat's neck, and we won't need to be afraid of her ever again. Now, who will volunteer to put the bell on the cat?"

Silence. Most of the mice looked down, hoping not to be noticed. Finally, the old mouse spoke up. "I knew it. It's easy to talk about a courageous idea, but acting on it is another matter!"

Cause and Effect

A cause makes something happen. The effect is what happens. When you read, notice cause and effect relationships. This will help you to understand how and why things occur.

1. Read the text. List three things people have done to cause harm to coral reefs.

   Cause: _____

   Cause: _____

   Cause: _____

2. What is the effect of the world's oceans becoming warmer on coral reefs?

   _____

   _____

3. Why should we be concerned about the health of coral reefs?

   _____

   _____

Critical Thinking

What could possibly happen if all the coral reefs died?

_____

_____

_____

Trouble in the Coral Reefs

For millions of years, there have been underwater ecosystems called *coral reefs*. They have provided homes and food for thousands of living things. Fish and sea birds live near the reefs. They share it with giant clams, sea turtles, crabs, starfish, and many others. Now these beautiful places are in danger. So are the sea plants and animals near them. Scientists blame it on people and pollution. We have ruined more than one-fourth of Earth's coral reefs. Unless things change, all of the remaining reefs may die.

sea turtle

Some people think that coral is stone because it is rough and hard, but that is not true. Coral is actually a tiny animal! Tiny coral polyps form coral reefs. They have many different colors. These colors come from the algae living in the coral. The algae are food for the coral polyps.

Billions of coral polyps stick together. New ones grow on the skeletons of dead coral. This happens year after year. Over thousands of years, the coral builds up a reef. The reef rises from the ocean floor and grows until it almost reaches the sea's surface.

red finger sponge

Unfortunately, people have harmed the coral reefs in multiple ways. They have broken off pieces to sell or keep for themselves. To catch fish, people have dropped sticks of dynamite into the water. This has blown up parts of reefs. Water pollution has caused the sea plants near coral reefs to overgrow, blocking the sunlight that the algae need to survive.

bleached coral

The worst problem the coral reefs face is that the world's oceans are getting warmer. Warm water kills the algae. When the algae die, the coral loses both its food and its color. The coral turns white and dies. Scientists call this process *coral bleaching*. The bleached part of a coral reef cannot recover.

Draw Conclusions

When you draw conclusions, you make decisions based on what you read. The information is not stated in the story. You have to figure it out from what is provided. If you need to, reread the story to decide the answers.

1. Read the text. Then complete this paragraph:

   A lake is _____ than a pond. As a result, the water in a lake is

   _____ at the bottom than at the surface. Also, plants cannot grow at

   the bottom of a _____ like they do at the bottom of a _____.

2. Draw a conclusion about how each of the following ponds form.

   a pond about a quarter mile from a river: _____

   _____

   a pond near a parking lot in a mall: _____

   _____

   a pond with a beaver den in the center: _____

   _____

Critical Thinking

What is one reason the author believes that springtime is the most interesting time at a pond?

_____

_____

_____

At the Pond

Ponds form in a variety of ways. People may use power equipment to dig a pond to collect water and prevent floods. A landslide may block a stream. Or a beaver may build a dam to block a stream on purpose. Some ponds form after a river overflows its banks each spring. When the river recedes, little ponds are left in the surrounding low areas. Other ponds are fed by springs of underground water. The water slowly bubbles up through the ground and keeps the ponds fresh and full.

Have you ever wondered about the difference between a pond and a lake? The difference is depth. A pond is so shallow that sunlight can reach to its bottom, allowing plants to grow there. In addition, a pond's water is the same temperature at the top and at the bottom.

Springtime at a pond is the most interesting time. Each spring, the pond receives more hours of sunlight each day than during the cold, bleak winter. That is when life in and around the pond starts to revive. First, the banks of the pond show signs of new life. Plants push up new sprouts. Some, like the water crowfoot, the yellow flag iris, and the spring lilac, burst into bloom. Their flowers add color to the grassy area surrounding the pond.

As the warmth of the sun spreads through the water, animal life begins to stir among the weeds at the bottom of the pond. Frogs, toads, fish, and salamanders mate and lay millions of eggs. Before long, the pond is seething with creatures. Newborn insects, snails, tadpoles, and tiny fish can be seen swarming in the water.

Draw Conclusions

When you draw conclusions, you make decisions based on what you read. The information is not stated in the story. You have to figure it out from what is provided. If you need to, reread the text to decide the answers.

1. Read the text. Where is the safest place to be during a blizzard? Explain.

   _____

2. What two factors make a blizzard worse than an ordinary snowstorm?

   _____

   _____

3. Suppose you are driving in a car when a blizzard occurs. Name one reason why you should get off the road.

   _____

   _____

4. Why did settlers sometimes freeze to death even though they had a rope between the house and the barn?

   _____

   _____

Critical Thinking

In 2006, the people in China and Japan knew about the coming blizzard. Why did the storm still cause trouble?

_____

_____

_____

BLIZZARD!

A blizzard is more than just a bad snowstorm. It's a powerful snowstorm with strong, cold winds. Blizzards usually come after a period of warm winter weather. In the Northern Hemisphere, a mass of cold air moves down from the Arctic Circle and meets the warmer air. The result is a heavy snowfall whipped around by bitter northerly winds of at least 35 miles per hour (56 kph) and temperatures of 20°F (–6.7°C) or lower. The blowing snow makes it hard to see even a foot or two ahead. The wind speed and cold create a dangerous condition called *wind chill*. Wind chill can cause hypothermia in people and animals. With hypothermia, the body's temperature drops until it freezes to death.

Today, weather reports warn about coming blizzards. In the past, these dangerous storms came with little warning. A huge blizzard in March 1888 covered the eastern United States, choking New York City. It took more than a week to dig out the city. During that time, many people froze to death.

Blizzards caused trouble for the settlers in the West, too. People had to rush to get themselves and their animals indoors. Otherwise, they would have died. It was risky to be out in a storm, yet someone had to feed the animals. So, people tacked one end of a rope to their barns. They nailed the other end of the rope to their houses. They went back and forth holding the rope. This kept them from getting lost in the blinding snow. Even so, sometimes people were found frozen just a few feet from their houses or barns.

A huge blizzard covered New York City in 1888.

A snowplow removes snow from a road.

Blizzards occur in the U.S. Northern Plains states, in eastern and central Canada, and in Russia. Blizzards also happen in the part of South America closest to the South Pole. The high winds can blow snow into huge drifts 15 feet (5 m) high. These snowdrifts often stop all travel. Schools and businesses close down for days. All the snow must be cleared away. During that time, snowplows may be the only traffic on the roads.

China and Japan experienced one of the worst blizzards in recorded history in January 2006. During nine days, it dumped 10 feet (3 m) of snow. The roofs of some homes actually collapsed beneath the weight of so much snow.

Infer

When you infer, you make decisions based on information you read. The information is not given. You have to figure it out from the information provided. Some people call this "reading between the lines." If you need to, reread the text to decide the answers.

1. Read the text. How many femurs does your skeleton have? _____

2. What is the purpose of the bones in your foot?

   _____

3. Which bone is not connected to any other bones in your body?

   _____

4. Think about each muscle. Then identify it as voluntary or involuntary.

   _____ thigh muscle

   _____ blood vessel muscles

   _____ facial muscles

   _____ muscles in your intestine

   _____ eye muscle

Critical Thinking

How did identifying which muscles were voluntary and which were involuntary help you to understand the information in the text?

_____

_____

_____

Your Skeleton and Muscles

Bones are inside every part of your body. The bones connect together to form your skeleton, which determines your size and shape. Each bone in your body has its own job. Some bones, such as your skull, are for protection. The skull protects your brain. Some bones, such as your ribs, give you shape. Ribs make the shape of your chest and protect your heart, lungs, stomach, and liver. Some bones, such as your femur (thigh bone), give you strength to stand and walk.

Bones may be soft on the inside, but they are hard on the outside. They are made from some of the same things you can find in rocks! These things are called *minerals*. Bones are also dry compared to the rest of the body. The majority of your body is made of water, but only a small part of your skeleton is.

All the bones of your skeleton are connected to each other, except for one. The thyroid bone, which is in your throat, is behind your tongue and above your Adam's apple. Muscles hold it in place.

Your muscles are the parts of the body that move bones and make your heart, lungs, and stomach work. Muscles are made up of elastic fibers. There are three kinds of muscle: skeletal, smooth, and cardiac. The skeletal muscles help your body move. You control these muscles in your arms, fingers, legs, and neck. Smooth muscles are in your digestive system and air passages. Smooth muscles also line the walls of blood vessels to make blood move. Cardiac muscle is just in your heart. It keeps your heart pumping every moment of your life. Smooth and cardiac muscles are involuntary muscles. This means that they do their jobs without you having to think about them.

There are more than 650 different muscles in your body. They make up a little less than half your total weight. This means that if you weigh 60 pounds (27.22 kg), your muscles weigh about 25 pounds (11.34 kg).

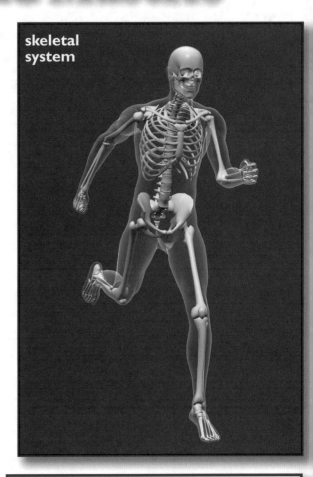

skeletal system

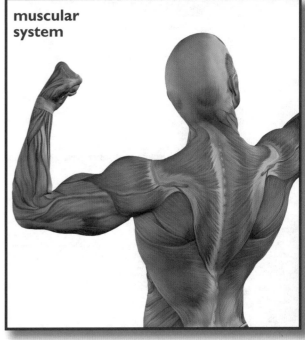

muscular system

Infer

1. Read the text. What can you tell about Sir Hubert's personality? Explain.

   _____

   _____

2. Is Princess Penelope aware of Sir Hubert's true feelings? Explain.

   _____

   _____

3. Do you think that Prince Tristan and the griffin have been honest with the princess? Explain.

   _____

   _____

Critical Thinking

Predict what might happen next in the story.

_____

_____

_____

DANGER FROM THE SKY

Sir Hubert had never seen the princess so serious. She was usually chatting wittily with the lords and ladies of the court or politely giving orders to the castle staff. Now she stood straight and tall with determination on her face. The tall knight felt sweat trickle down his spine.

"Sir Knight," she spoke stiffly, "a griffin has been spotted making its way here. Gather your soldiers and prepare to defend the castle!"

Sir Hubert moved quickly to arrange his archers along the castle parapet. The men had barely reached their position when the griffin appeared in the sky! As the enormous animal streaked toward them, the archers readied their shots.

"Hold your arrows!" The cry came from the princess. "Look! There is a man riding the creature's back!"

The griffin landed on the roof of the castle. Prince Tristan leaped lightly from his mount. "Princess Penelope, please forgive me, but I couldn't wait to tell you my news! King Griffin has agreed to an alliance!"

As the archers peered suspiciously at the monstrous lion-bird, Sir Hubert fought an overwhelming sense of panic. There was tension in the air. A flash of indecision crossed the princess' face. Then she smiled and moved gracefully toward the creature. She curtsied regally and said, "Our kingdom welcomes friendship with the noble Griffins!"

Sir Hubert held his breath, unsure what the creature's response would be. The griffin hesitated, then placed one great paw in front of the other and dipped its head. Princess Penelope smiled and said, "Let us have a celebration feast! Prince Tristan and King Griffin, you will be my guests of honor!"

Summarize

To summarize, you tell only the most important information from the text.

1. Read the text. Write the main idea in the center of the web. Then, in each of the six boxes, write relevant words or phrases.

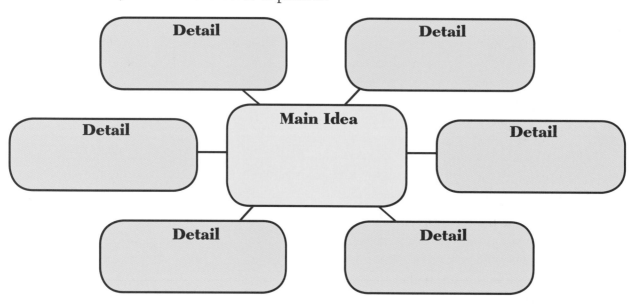

Detail

Detail

Detail

Main Idea

Detail

Detail

Detail

2. Use the information in the graphic organizer to write a summary of the text.

_____

_____

_____

Critical Thinking

How does writing a summary of a text help you to concentrate on its main idea?

_____

_____

_____

Ballet

Long, long ago, the first true ballet was performed in France. Ballet is a dance performed with special body movements and positions. It usually tells a story. Ballet actually began in Italy. However, the first ballet school was in France, and all the words used in ballet are French. The French turned ballet into the beautiful art form we know today.

Ballerinas are girls. Boys who dance are danseurs. Ballet dancers may begin their training with classes at the age of three or four. They are introduced to music and the basic positions of ballet. By 11 or 12, ballet dancers may have daily lessons. They must train very hard. If they have enough desire and talent, they may be fortunate enough to join a professional ballet company by seventeen or eighteen.

Even during their free time, ballet dancers often have ballet on their minds. They are athletes, and they always want to be strong and fit. They enjoy the control that ballet gives them over their bodies. It lets them move and pose in ways that are nearly impossible for people who are not ballet dancers.

Summarize

To summarize, you tell only the most important information from the text.

1. Read the text. Beginning with the paragraph beneath the first heading, write a summary sentence for each paragraph.

Paragraph 1: _____

_____

Paragraph 2: _____

_____

Paragraph 3: _____

_____

Paragraph 4: _____

_____

Paragraph 5: _____

_____

Critical Thinking

How do summary sentences help you to understand text?

_____

_____

_____

ANCIENT GREECE

Greece is located on the southern tip of Europe. It borders the Aegean, Adriatic, and Mediterranean seas. Greece has a large mainland surrounded by many smaller islands. It is a hot, dry country with mountain ranges.

Religion

Ancient Greek life centered on religion. Greeks worshipped many gods and goddesses. The Greeks thought that the gods controlled every part of people's lives. Big decisions about war and marriage were made only after checking with the gods. Even small decisions were made this way. Poseidon was the god of the seas and rivers. Apollo controlled the sun and light. Aphrodite was the goddess of love and beauty. Athena was the goddess of war and wisdom.

Art and Theater

The ancient Greeks made statues and beautiful temples for their gods. Huge wall paintings called murals decorated these buildings. Although the ruins of these buildings remain, the paint wore away long ago.

In 534 B.C., the first public plays were held in Athens. They were performed in open-air theaters shaped like semicircles. Seats were built into the hillsides. Early Greek plays had religious themes. Later plays began to deal with politics. Some ancient Greek plays are still performed today.

Science and Medicine

The ancient Greeks were interested in science. They made advances in biology, mathematics, astronomy, and geography. They based what they knew on what they observed in the world. They were the first people in Europe to do this.

Medicine was an important science for the Greeks. At first, they believed that illnesses were punishment from the gods. Sanctuaries were built all over Greece. These holy places honored the god of medicine. People would spend the night at a sanctuary to pray for a cure. Later, the Greeks came up with treatments for diseases. A Greek doctor named Hippocrates designed many of these treatments. He is called the Father of Modern Medicine.

Paraphrase

When you paraphrase, you restate the information in a text in your own words.

1. How many paragraphs are there in this text? _____

2. Read the text. Write one sentence to paraphrase (sum up) each paragraph.
   (Hint: In one of the paragraphs, a topic sentence does this for you.)

   _____

   _____

   _____

   _____

   _____

3. Paraphrase the whole text in your own words in two sentences.

   _____

   _____

   _____

   _____

Critical Thinking

How did summing up the text in your own words help you to understand what you read?

_____

_____

_____

"Green" Cell Phones

When cell phones first came out, they were expensive and big. Often it was hard to get a signal. Many people bought them just for road emergencies. They kept them in their cars.

Now, more people have cell phones than landlines (phones in their homes). Advances in cell phones have made them smaller while allowing users to text as well as talk. Today's phones have multiple uses. They can access the Internet so users can send and receive email. Users can get maps and directions and read the news. They can listen to music. Most cell phones have a built-in camera, too.

Many companies are working to improve cell phones even more. One cell phone maker is currently working on a phone that runs on soda! Nokia is testing a phone that would turn the sugars in soda into electrical power. It says this new "bio-battery" would be safer for the environment. That's because regular batteries contain toxic metals—like lead—that are harmful to the environment if they are not disposed of in the right way. Right now few people dispose of their cell phone batteries properly.

The new soda batteries would be biodegradable. This means they that would decay naturally. Plus, they could have an added bonus. The company says that they should last three times longer than current cell phone batteries!

Paraphrase

When you paraphrase, you restate the information in a text in your own words.

1. How many paragraphs are there in this text? _____

2. Read the text. Write one sentence to paraphrase (sum up) each paragraph. This text does not have any topic sentences, so you will have to use your own words.

    _____

    _____

    _____

    _____

    _____

3. Paraphrase the whole text in your own words in two sentences.

    _____

    _____

    _____

    _____

Critical Thinking

How did summing up the text in your own words help you to understand what you read?

_____

_____

_____

Roberto Clemente

Roberto Clemente grew up in Carolina, Puerto Rico. His parents always told him that they wanted him to be a good man. From an early age, he loved baseball. He played every chance he could get. While listening to the radio, he would squeeze a ball to build up the muscles in his throwing arm. He would bounce a rubber ball off the wall to practice catching. He and his friends could not afford to buy real baseballs. So, they made their own out of old golf balls, string, and tape.

As Roberto grew older, he practiced even more. He became an excellent baseball player. In high school, the Brooklyn Dodgers offered Roberto a job, but he did not accept. His father said he had to finish school first. After Roberto graduated, he went to Montreal, Canada. He played on a farm team there. Some pro teams came to watch him play. When the Pittsburgh Pirates asked him to play right field for their team, Roberto accepted.

Roberto Clemente
Pittsburgh Pirates

MLB PHOTOS / GETTY IMAGES

Roberto Clemente

As a Pirate, Roberto was on the team when it won the World Series twice. He was the Most Valuable Player in the 1971 World Series. He had more than 3,000 hits in his career.

As a champion, Roberto never forgot his fans. He donated money to needy people. He spent time visiting sick children. When an earthquake struck Nicaragua, he spent the Christmas holiday collecting supplies for the victims. He boarded a plane to fly from Puerto Rico to Nicaragua on December 31, 1972, to deliver the supplies. Sadly, shortly after the plane took off, it crashed. Roberto and everyone else on board died.

Three months later, he was voted into the Baseball Hall of Fame. Roberto's parents wanted him to be a good man. Roberto proved to be a *great* man.

Table of Contents

A table of contents appears at the start of a nonfiction book. It lists the chapters that are in the book. By scanning the table of contents, you can tell if the book might answer a question you have.

1. Scan the table of contents. How many chapters are in this book? _____

2. Read the table of contents. About how many pages are in this book? _____

3. On what page would you probably find the definition of the Cold War? _____

4. In which chapter would you read about Chinese immigrants?

_____

5. Write the name(s) of the chapter(s) about World War II.

_____

_____

_____

Critical Thinking

How does a book's table of contents differ from its index?

_____

_____

_____

THE TWENTIETH CENTURY

Table of Contents

Table of Contents

A table of contents appears at the start of a nonfiction book. It lists the chapters that are in the book. By scanning the table of contents, you can tell if the book might answer a question you have.

1. Scan the table of contents. How many chapters are in this book? _____

2. Read the table of contents. About how many pages are in this book? _____

3. On what page would you be most likely to find the definition of team-building activities? _____

4. In which chapter would you read about how to join a team?

   _____

5. Write the name(s) of the chapter(s) about how to lead a team.

   _____

Critical Thinking

When would you use a table of contents?

_____

_____

_____

Teamwork

Table of Contents

Index

An index is always on the last pages of a nonfiction book. It is a list of important topics that are covered in the book. Specific words and ideas are given their own listings. If you want to see if a word is mentioned in a book, use the index.

1. Scan the index. How are the entries listed—in the order in which they appear in the book or alphabetically? How do you know?

   _____

   _____

2. Read the index. On what page would you find information about Arabic numerals?

3. If you turned to page 17, what would you read about?

   _____

4. What is the first page to which you would turn to read about kanji characters? _____

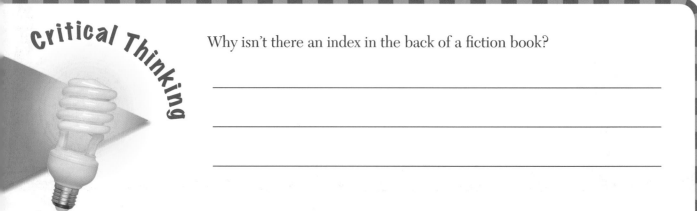

Critical Thinking

Why isn't there an index in the back of a fiction book?

_____

_____

_____

History of Schools

Index

Index

An index is always on the last pages of a nonfiction book. It is a list of important topics that are covered in the book. Specific words and ideas are given their own listings. If you want to see if a word is mentioned in a book, use the index.

1. Scan the index. How are the entries listed—in the order in which they appear in the book or alphabetically? How do you know?

    _____

    _____

2. Read the index. On what pages would you find information about scrubland?

    _____

3. If you turned to page 14, what would you read about?

    _____

4. If you wanted to learn about wetlands, what is the first page would you turn to?

    _____

Critical Thinking

How does a book's index differ from its table of contents?

_____

_____

_____

Index

Glossary

A glossary is like a very short dictionary placed in the back of a nonfiction book. The glossary lists the definition of important words used in the book. If you are reading and don't understand a word, turn to the glossary.

1. Read the glossary. What is the definition of *coastal*?

   _____

2. Which word means "particles of sediment"?

   _____

3. What is the difference between freshwater and groundwater?

   _____

   _____

4. Use the word *erosion* in a sentence.

   _____

   _____

Critical Thinking

When would you use a glossary?

_____

_____

_____

Glossary

amphibian—a type of animal that spends part or all of its life living in water

coastal—located along a coast; of the shore or coast

decay—to rot and break down into raw materials; decompose

erosion—the wearing away of land by water and wind

filter—a device that allows liquid or gas to pass through but keeps out dirt and other particles

freshwater—water from rivers, streams, and other inland sources that contains no salt

groundwater—water from beneath the earth's surface

habitat—a place where groups of the same kinds of plants and animals live together at the same time

organism—a living thing that has the ability to act by itself

pollution—chemicals or materials that make water or air dirty

silt—very small particles of sediment, smaller than sand

tidal—relating to the tides (the change of sea level from high to low and back again, caused by gravity)

wetlands—a low area, such as a marsh or swamp, filled with moisture and many plants and animals

Glossary

A glossary is like a very short dictionary placed in the back of a nonfiction book. The glossary lists the definition of important words used in the book. If you are reading and don't understand a word, turn to the glossary.

1. Scan the glossary. You will see some words you don't know. List two below.

   _____   _____

2. Read the text. Write the definition for one of the words you listed above.

   _____

   _____

3. What do the initials ATM stand for?

   _____

4. Name the two words that mean "to trade."

   _____

Critical Thinking

How does a glossary differ from an index?

_____

_____

_____

History of Money

Glossary

account—a record of money received or paid out

automatic teller machine (ATM)—a machine that lets you deposit or withdraw money from your account, even if the bank is closed or you're far away from home

bank note—a paper that may be used as money

barter—to trade goods or services for other goods or services

bit—a piece cut from a Spanish dollar known as a piece of eight

counterfeit—to make a false copy of printed money in order to deceive

credit card—a plastic card with which one can buy things now, promising to pay later

currency—the basic unit of money for a nation

debit card—a plastic card with which a person can move money directly from the person's bank account into another's account

deposit—to place for safekeeping in a bank

economy—the system of money, products, and labor in a country

euro—a common currency adopted by twelve European nations in 2002

exchange—to trade

exchange rate—how one currency compares to another

Federal Reserve Note—the official name of a U.S. dollar bill

interest—money paid to a lender (account holder) or money received from a borrower

mint—to stamp a design on a coin

wampum—belts made of beads or shells used as money by early American Indians

withdraw—to take away

Answer Key

Preview, p. 8

1. Answers will vary. Sample: I know that the Egyptian pyramids were built a very long time ago.
2. Answers will vary. Sample: The students wanted to know the exact size of the pyramid.
3. Answers will vary. Accept any two facts about pyramids from the text.

Critical Thinking answers will vary. Sample: Previewing the text helped me to understand it because I could think about what I already knew about the ancient Egyptians and pyramids.

Preview, p. 10

1. Answers will vary. Sample: Accept any two: Cleopatra, Julius Caesar, Mark Antony, Octavian
2. Answers will vary. Sample: Student must write the two names not written in #1.
3. 4, 1, 3, 2

Critical Thinking answers will vary. Sample: Previewing the text let me know who would be mentioned.

Predict, p. 12

1. Diego Rivera's profession is an artist.
2. Answers will vary. Sample: The title names a person, and there are dates mentioned, so I think it will be nonfiction.
3. Answers will vary. Sample: The word *eccentric* probably means unusual.
4. Answers will vary. Sample: No, Diego Rivera died in 1957 because his birth and death dates are in parentheses immediately following his name.
5. Answers will vary. If student writes yes, make sure the predictions in 1–4 really were correct. If the answer is no, the student needs to provide an explanation.

Critical Thinking answers will vary. Sample: Making predictions helped me to understand what I read because I wanted to know how Diego Rivera created murals.

Predict, p. 14

1. Answers will vary. Sample: I think that it will be fiction because the text doesn't include photographs.
2. Answers will vary. Sample: *Disfigured* means crippled, ugly, or damaged.
3. Answers will vary. Sample: Moonlight stays hidden beneath the bearskin because she wants a man to fall in love with her personality and not with her beauty.
4. Answers will vary. Student needs to answer whether he or she made accurate predictions and give an explanation.

Critical Thinking answers will vary. Sample: I think that Moonlight will be forced to drop her bearskin and will be beautiful.

Prior Knowledge, p. 16

1. Answers will vary. Sample: Accept any two facts about natural forces.
2. Answers will vary. Sample: When I throw a ball in the air, gravity pulls it to the ground.
3. Answers will vary. Sample: I wear cleats when I play soccer to keep me from slipping in the grass.
4. Answers will vary. Sample: The captions helped me to understand an example of each natural force.

Critical Thinking answers will vary. Sample: Thinking about what I already knew about natural forces helped me to understand the new information about inertia.

Prior Knowledge, p. 18

1. Answers will vary. Accept any two facts about electricity.
2. Answers will vary. Accept any two facts about magnets.
3. Answers will vary. Sample: Static electricity made me get shocked when I touched the car door.
4. iron
5. Answers will vary. Sample: Magnets are attracted to the front of my refrigerator.

Critical Thinking answers will vary. Sample: If my mom doesn't use a dryer sheet, the clothes are affected by static electricity.

Answer Key *(cont.)*

Set a Purpose, p. 20

1. Answers will vary. Sample: How do unseen volcanoes build new land?

2. Answers will vary. Sample: What land has been formed by volcanoes?

3. Answers will vary. Sample: Unseen volcanoes build new land by erupting on the ocean floor. Over many years, the lava cools and builds up until the volcano actually bursts through the surface as a new island.

4. Answers will vary. Accept any fact about volcanoes from the text.

Critical Thinking answers will vary. Sample: No, I can look it up online, in an encyclopedia, or in a library book.

Set a Purpose, p. 22

1. Answers will vary. Sample: Where is Niagara Falls?

2. Answers will vary. Sample: How tall is Niagara Falls?

3. Answers will vary. Sample: Niagara Falls is located off the Niagara River between the border of Canada and the United States.

4. Answers will vary. Sample: Niagara Falls is constantly eroding. That means that the falls eat away at the rocks.

Critical Thinking answers will vary. Sample: No, I can look it up online, in an encyclopedia, or in a library book.

Ask Questions, p. 24

1. Answers will vary. Sample: I think that this text will be about creating a school website.

2. Answers will vary. Sample: Sarah asked her teacher if their class could update the school calendar on the website.

3. Answers will vary. Sample: Sarah asked the principal if her class could redo the whole website.

4. Answers will vary. Sample: The principal agreed because he saw that Sarah's class did a good job with the school calendar.

5. Answers will vary. Sample: Do you think people will hire you if they know you are just 13 years old?

Critical Thinking answers will vary. Sample: I liked the question-and-answer format because it was like listening to a conversation.

Ask Questions, p. 26

1. Answers will vary. Sample: The text will be about forms of energy.

2. Answers will vary. Accept any question.

3. Answers will vary but should be a reasonable answer to the question written for #2.

4. Answers will vary. Accept any question about the topic.

Critical Thinking answers will vary. Sample: I will look up the answer online.

Make Connections, p. 28

1. Answers will vary. Sample: I wanted to fit in with my classmates at my new school.

2. Answers will vary. Sample: Yes, I love roller coasters because I like to go fast and be a little scared.

3. Answers will vary. Sample: He would have felt embarrassed in front of his brother and friends.

4. Answers will vary. Sample: The writer went on all the same rides as the older kids and talked to them.

Critical Thinking answers will vary. Sample: Making connections to my own life helped me to understand how the writer felt and how much he wanted to be accepted by Luis's friends.

Make Connections, p. 30

1. Answers will vary. Sample: I was "the new kid" when my family moved to a new city.

2. Answers will vary. Sample: I'm like Connor because I'm very nervous and shy when I meet new people.

3. Answers will vary. Sample: I wanted to make a good impression at baseball tryouts but I kept striking out.

Critical Thinking answers will vary. Sample: Making connections to my own life helped me to understand how nervous Connor was and how embarrassed he was when he mixed up right and left.

Answer Key (cont.)

Context Clues, p. 32

1. Answers will vary. Sample: The word *despised* means "hated." I know because it talks about how tests made Allen feel ill and he says that he hates tests.
2. Answers will vary. Sample: The word *astute* means "able to figure out." I know because the teacher figured out that the kids needed help to improve their test scores.
3. Answers will vary. Sample: An *eye opener* is a surprising idea that a person hasn't had before. I know because it says Allen had never thought this way before.

Critical Thinking answers will vary. Sample: Using context clues helps me because I can use sentences and words to figure out the meaning of unknown words.

Context Clues, p. 34

1. Answers will vary. Sample: *Agriculture* is farming. I know because George was a greenhouse director and he taught farmers.
2. Answers will vary. Sample: Another word for *appointed* is assigned. I know because George became head of the college's Department of Agriculture.
3. Answers will vary. Sample: The term *bumper crop* means a huge harvest, more than anyone expected. I know because it says nobody knew what to do with all the peanuts.

Critical Thinking answers will vary. Sample: Using context clues helped me to understand what agriculture means. This word is important to understanding the whole text.

Visualize, p. 36

1. Pictures will vary but should show a flatboat, lobster traps, or a man baiting a lobster trap.
2. Pictures will vary but should show a lobster with eggs under the curve of her tail or eggs floating on the sea's surface.
3. Pictures will vary but should show tiny lobsters, adult lobsters, or a lobster in a trap.

Critical Thinking answers will vary. Sample: Picturing what was in the text helped me to understand about the different stages of development for lobsters.

Visualize, p. 38

1. Pictures will vary but should show Sofia removing her flip-flops or creeping up the stairs.
2. Pictures will vary but should show Sofia tiptoeing down the hall, opening her parents' bedroom door, or moving toward to the closet.
3. Pictures will vary but should show Sofia getting the box from the top shelf of the closet, eagerly opening it, or looking shocked as she reads an unfolded note.

Critical Thinking answers will vary. Sample: It was like making a movie in my mind, so I saw the story unfold as it happened.

Story Elements, p. 40

1. Maritza, Chloe, Cynthia
2. Answers will vary. Sample: It is modern times. The first part of the story occurs in school, but the most important part occurs at a jewelry rack in a mall store.
3. Answers will vary. Sample: Maritza wants to be friends with Chloe, yet she sees that Chloe's sister Cynthia stole something.
4. Answers will vary. Sample: No, the conflict is not resolved by the end. We are left wondering what Maritza will do next.

Critical Thinking answers will vary. Sample: I think that Maritza will try to stop Cynthia, and they will get into an argument.

Story Elements, p. 42

1. Jennifer, Twila
2. Answers will vary. Sample: The setting is at night in an art museum.
3. Answers will vary. Sample: Twila wants to look at a painting, but the girls aren't supposed to leave the room. Jennifer is unsure whether she should follow Twila.
4. Answers will vary. Sample: The conflict is mostly resolved because Jennifer decides to go find Twila. However, we don't know if they make it back to the room without being caught.

Critical Thinking answers will vary. Sample: I think that Ms. Lathy will wake up and catch the girls. They will get in trouble.

Answer Key *(cont.)*

Plot, p. 44

1. Answers will vary. Sample: Raj is a boy who is really interested in cars.
2. Answers will vary. Sample: Raj's problem is that he desperately wants to go to the big auto show, but his mom always says it is too far away.
3. Answers will vary. Sample: I think that Raj will open the envelope and discover the tickets.

Critical Thinking answers will vary. Sample: Writers include plot twists in their stories to keep a reader interested and guessing what will happen.

Plot, p. 46

1. Answers will vary. Sample: Zoomer is a flying robot.
2. Answers will vary. Sample: Johan is worried that he will be separated from Zoomer.
3. Answers will vary. Sample: No, the problem is not solved by the end, but we get the idea that the team will win the race and stay together.

Critical Thinking answers will vary. Sample: Stories wouldn't be as interesting if plots were solved quickly.

Characters, p. 48

1. Answers will vary. Sample: strong, determined, greedy, cautious
2. Answers will vary. Sample: Captain Butterbeard's crew is a rough crowd that would turn on him and take the prizes for themselves.

Critical Thinking answers will vary. Student must state a character that could be added to this story and what this character would say or do.

Characters, p. 50

1. Answers will vary. Sample: King Midas
2. Answers will vary. Sample: King Midas is greedy.
3. Answers will vary. Sample: King Midas wants to get rid of his gift or he will starve to death.
4. Answers will vary. Sample: King Midas learned that gold is not the most valuable thing.

Critical Thinking answers will vary. Sample: The other characters were not really central to the plot so the author didn't include more information about them.

Title and Headings, p. 52

1. Answers will vary. Sample: I think it will be about a race across crates.
2. Answers will vary. Sample:
   When and Where: August 15
   Race Rules: Racers must cross 50 crates to the end and back to win.
   What You Need: sneakers
   Who Can Enter?: all kids ages 17 and under

Critical Thinking answers will vary. Sample: The headings make it easy to find specific information quickly.

Title and Headings, p. 54

1. Answers will vary. Sample: The text will be about the human body.
2. Heading: The Human Circulatory System; Purpose: It moves blood all through the body, bringing fresh oxygen and removing carbon dioxide.
   Heading: The Human Respiratory System; Purpose: It adds oxygen to the blood and removes carbon dioxide.
3. Answers will vary. Sample: The illustrations show the systems that the headings and text discuss.

Critical Thinking answers will vary. Sample: The writer used headings to help readers to focus on one body system at a time.

Typeface and Captions, p. 56

1. boldface
2. menagerie, endangered, captivity
3. Answers will vary. Sample: Those words are set in a special typeface because they are key vocabulary terms.
4. Answers will vary. Sample: The three words in the special typeface are used in the captions on the page.

Critical Thinking answers will vary. Sample: The pictures helped to show the meanings of the words.

Answer Key *(cont.)*

Typeface and Captions, p. 58

1. italics
2. Answers will vary. Sample: The words in italics are key vocabulary terms that are explained in the text.
3. Answers will vary. Samples: absorption: when light falls on a piece of furniture and the wood absorbs most of the light; refraction: as light travels through a sliding glass door, it bends; reflection: you can see the sky in a puddle on the ground.

Critical Thinking answers will vary. Sample: The captions explain which example of light each photo illustrates.

Graphics, p. 60

1. Thomas Edison
2. It is a time line.
3. phonograph, LP, cassette tapes, compact discs (CDs), MP3 player, digital audio
4. Answers will vary. Sample: The terms are boldfaced in the text because they are included on the time line so you can see how each item looks and when it was invented.

Critical Thinking answers will vary. Samples: The time line helped me to understand because I had never seen a phonograph or an LP, and it gave specific dates when the things were invented.

Graphics, p. 62

1. Answers will vary. Sample: Damage from an earthquake is shown in the bottom photo. The photo on the left shows a fault line.
2. Answers will vary. Sample: The drawing shows how seismic waves move outward from the epicenter of a quake.
3. epicenter, seismic waves, tsunami
4. Answers will vary. Sample: These words are italicized because they are key terms essential to understanding the text topic.

Critical Thinking answers will vary. Sample: It helped me to understand what an epicenter was and how seismic waves extend in all directions from it.

Topic Sentences, p. 64

1. Earth's spinning causes a cycle of changing seasons.
2. Answers will vary. Sample: Earth makes one revolution around the sun each year while at the same time it rotates on its axis once each day.
3. Since Earth is tilted, the sun's most direct rays strike Earth in different places as the planet revolves around the sun.
4. It would be winter in the Northern Hemisphere.

Critical Thinking answers will vary. Sample: The next time I read a nonfiction text, I will use the topic sentences to help me understand the main idea of each paragraph.

Topic Sentences, p. 66

1. Firefighters are always busy.
2. Firefighters take turns doing the chores at the station.
3. In addition to fires, they rush to help in many different emergencies.
4. Firefighters keep busy even when there are no emergencies.

Critical Thinking answers will vary. Sample: The topic sentences summarize the main idea of each paragraph, so if I wrote each one down, I would have a summary of the text.

Main Idea, p. 68

1. Milo is the main character in the story.
2. Answers will vary. Sample: He is determined to kill the Pink Jingly Puff Ball.
3. Answers will vary. Sample:

   Main Idea: Milo stalks, attacks, and believes he has killed the Pink Jingly Puff Ball.

   Details: Milo's body tenses and his eyes lock on his prey; The fully alert hunter slowly begins his approach; He hides behind the cedar chest to await an attack opportunity; Inch by inch Milo creeps across the carpet; He springs full force on the Pink Jingly Puff Ball and shakes it; When the puff ball shows no sign of life, Milo believes he has killed it and is pleased with himself.

Critical Thinking answers will vary. Sample: The author wants readers to use context clues and the picture to figure out that Milo is a cat.

Answer Key (cont.)

Main Idea, p. 70

1. Answers will vary. Sample: My mom bought a pink glowing light stick for me at an amusement park.
2. Answers will vary. Sample: The main idea of this text is how a light stick works.
3. Answers will vary. Sample: Details: A light stick is made of plastic filled with hydrogen peroxide; Inside is a small glass tube filled with phenyl oxalate ester; When you bend the light stick, the glass tube breaks; When the two chemicals mix, it causes a reaction called *chemiluminesence*, which makes the stick glow; Dyes within the stick make different-colored lights.

Critical Thinking answers will vary. Sample: Finding the main idea of fiction differs because the story will not clearly state a main idea in one or two sentences.

Details, p. 72

1. Max, Abby
2. Answers will vary. Sample: Max has a scary dream that Abby and he are attacked by a giant red ant at their campsite.
3. Answers will vary. Sample: Details: Max sees a blister on the tree's bark next to where Abby and the ant are struggling; Max grabs the camp ax and throws it at the tree, hitting the blister; Amber-colored liquid spews all over the ant; Max pulls hard, and Abby flies to one side; When the ant grabs Max's arms, it snaps its menacing pincers at his face.

Critical Thinking answers will vary. Sample: I think it is easier to find the main idea and details in nonfiction because the structure of nonfiction text makes it easier to find details in the paragraphs.

Details, p. 74

1. Answers will vary. Sample: Main Idea: The Johnson Space Center in Houston, Texas, trains astronauts and directs space missions.
2. Answers will vary. Sample: Details: The center opened in 1961 and is named for former President Lyndon B. Johnson; In the Mission Control Center, people direct the space missions by talking to astronauts in space; Astronauts study to learn the skills they'll need in their space travel; Astronauts train with the people they will be with in space.

Critical Thinking answers will vary. Sample: The details in fiction are not necessarily true, but the details in nonfiction are facts that can be proven.

Main Idea and Details, p. 76

1. Answers will vary. Sample: Main Ideas:

   Paragraph 1: Confucius was a Chinese philosopher who lived long ago and whose influence continues today.

   Paragraph 2: Confucius devoted his life to thinking of ways to improve the lives of the poor and to ending wars.

   Paragraph 3: Confucius started a school where both nobles and peasants could learn.

   Paragraph 4: Confucius taught his students that the government should help everyone have good lives.

   Paragraph 5: Confucius changed the world.

2. Answers will vary. Sample: Details:

   Paragraph 1: His teachings changed Chinese culture.

   Paragraph 2: Confucius read a lot and wanted things to improve.

   Paragraph 3: Confucius knew that education could make people equal.

   Paragraph 4: He wanted rulers to earn their power by being concerned for the people.

   Paragraph 5: In addition to China, other societies have adopted Confucius's ideas

Critical Thinking answers will vary. Sample: I looked for which details best supported the main idea and included those.

Chronological Order, p. 78

1. Answers will vary. Sample: On the first day, each athlete made a vow to compete fairly, and animals were sacrificed to Zeus.
2. 4, 1, 5, 2, 3
3. Answers will vary. Sample: first, second, third

Critical Thinking answers will vary. Sample: Authors write events in chronological order because it makes the most sense to tell a story from beginning to end.

Answer Key *(cont.)*

Chronological Order, p. 80

1. 2, 3, 4, 1
2. 1743: born on April 13; 1760: goes to the College of William and Mary; 1770: has Monticello built when Shadwell burns down; 1776: writes the Declaration of Independence; 1801: becomes third president of the United States

Critical Thinking answers will vary. Sample: I would include my birthday, the day I met my best friend, and when I started playing football.

Logical Order, p. 82

1. Answers will vary. Sample: Step 1: Buy or make a bin without a lid and choose a spot in your yard to put it; Step 2: Throw kitchen scraps and grass clippings into the pile but no cheese, meat, or animal fat; Step 3: Twice a month, use a shovel to dig up the pile and turn it over.
2. Answers will vary. Sample: First, buy or make a bin to put in your yard. Next, add kitchen scraps and plant matter to the pile. Then use a shovel to turn the pile about twice a month. Last, the material will become humus that you can spread on your garden.

Critical Thinking answers will vary. Sample: It's a good idea to create a compost pile and recycle as much as we can to keep trash from piling up.

Logical Order, p. 84

1. Answers will vary. Sample: Aunt Emilia doesn't think hydroponics will work.
2. one
3. Answers will vary. Sample: Vermiculite can be purchased at a gardening store.
4. Seven steps need to be done to get the project started.
5. The most time will pass after step 7.

Critical Thinking answers will vary. Sample: Aunt Emilia now knows that hydroponics works well.

Fact and Opinion, p. 86

1. Answers will vary. Sample: No, every student will not be delighted. Some students may actually hate the changes because people's tastes differ.
2. F, O, F, F, O
3. Answers will vary. Sample: It is impossible to know if this quote is a fact or an opinion. We don't know if a study was conducted to find out this information.

Critical Thinking answers will vary. Sample: Amy put her own opinions into the newscast when she says that chicken nuggets are terrible. Everyone may not feel this way.

Fact and Opinion, p. 88

1. Answers will vary. Sample: Accept any one of these facts: Picasso was born in 1881 in Malaga, Spain; At a young age, his artistic talent was recognized as extraordinary; At 15, Picasso was admitted to the Royal Academy of Art in Barcelona, Spain; At age 19, Picasso moved to France.
2. Answers will vary. Sample: He worked in ceramics and sculpture and made collages.
3. O, O, F, O, F

Critical Thinking answers will vary. Sample: Cubism is very different from anything that people had seen before Picasso created it.

Answer Key (cont.)

Proposition and Support, p. 90

1. Answers will vary. Sample: I think the proposition will be that the author wants there to be less school garbage.
2. Answers will vary. Sample: The writer says that a lot of recyclable items are being thrown in the trash at school.
3. Answers will vary. Sample: Put recycling bins next to the trash cans; Put recycling bins for paper in every classroom.
4. Answers will vary. Sample: These phrases tell me it is a problem and solution text: "one solution to the problem," "another solution," "if all these suggestions were implemented."

Critical Thinking answers will vary. Sample: Using recycling bins would work the best because it would be easier than people bringing lunch boxes or thermoses since some kids may not have these items.

Proposition and Support, p. 92

1. Answers will vary. Sample: I think that the author's proposition will be that we need to do something to help reindeer survive.
2. Answers will vary. Sample: Global warming has caused freezing rain that makes it hard for reindeer and caribou to eat enough lichen.
3. Answers will vary. Sample: The writer wants me to do what I can to fight global warming. The writer wants me to change my habits so they are more Earth-friendly.

Critical Thinking answers will vary. Sample: Yes, the writer persuaded me that I can do things—even minor things—that will help to reduce global warming.

Author's Purpose, p. 94

1. Answers will vary. Sample: Eddie wrote this email to apologize and to explain that he only borrowed Jared's bike and meant to return it.
2. Answers will vary. Sample: Eddie hopes that Jared will forgive him and they can continue their friendship.
3. Answers will vary. Sample: Eddie chose to write an email rather than talk to Jared because he didn't want to get distracted or forget what to say.

Critical Thinking answers will vary. Sample: I think Jared will forgive Eddie.

Author's Purpose, p. 96

1. Answers will vary. Sample: The author wrote this text to give the reader facts about Saturn.
2. Answers will vary. Sample: The author would feel excited about visiting Saturn. I know because the writer says he or she wants to go camping there.
3. Answers will vary. Sample: The author used this format to tell the reader about Saturn because it is more interesting than listing facts.

Critical Thinking answers will vary. Sample: I think I might read something like this in a kids' magazine because they like to put an interesting spin on factual information.

Compare and Contrast, p. 98

1.

Softball Facts	Dance Facts
• great exercise	• great exercise
• her best friend, Isabella, is catcher	• makes her stronger and more flexible
• time is evenly split between practices and games	• more time spent practicing than performing
• crowd roars when someone gets a homerun	

2. Answers will vary; student must state at least one interest, hobby, or sport.
3. Answers will vary but must explain which one is top priority and why.

Critical Thinking answers will vary. Sample: I predict that Jasmine will choose softball because she named more details about it.

Answer Key (cont.)

Compare and Contrast, p. 100

1. Answers will vary. Sample: African Savanna: Zebras, elephants, lions, and leopards live there; It is covered in grass with scattered trees and bushes; It has a wet season and a dry season.

   Sahara Desert: Gazelles, antelopes, jackals, foxes, badgers, and hyenas live there; It is covered in sand dunes, mountains, steppes; It is very dry; It can be very hot during the day and cold at night; Grasses, shrubs, and trees only grow near oases and along rivers.

   both: located in Africa; have many living things

2. the Serengeti Plain

3. Answers will vary. Sample: The savanna is mostly warm and dry with a rainy season, while the desert is always hot and dry during the day and can be very cold at night.

Critical Thinking answers will vary. Sample: I would rather visit the grasslands because there are lots of trees, water, and grass.

Classify, p. 102

1.

Sweet	Sour	Salty	Bitter
cookies cupcake bananas	lemons grapefruit dill pickles limes	pretzels potato chips crackers	coffee beans unsweetened cocoa

2. Answers will vary. Sample: It's hard to taste when you have a bad cold because you need your nose in order to taste.

Critical Thinking answers will vary. Sample: The taste my tongue likes best is salty because I like chips, peanuts, and other salty things.

Classify, p. 104

1. Answers will vary. Sample:

Boy	Materials Used at the Library	Materials Checked Out to Take Home
Andy	baseball magazine	two books and a movie about baseball
Kyle	graphic novels/comics about spies	three spy novels, two graphic novels, and two movies with spies/chase scenes
Colby	magazine about sharks	book about spiders, book about snakes, and film about sharks

2. Kyle; explanations will vary. Sample: I can tell because he's really into spy novels and graphic novels/comics.

Critical Thinking answers will vary. Sample: I like to check out books on CD so I can listen to them while my family drives to my grandmother's house.

Cause and Effect, p. 106

1. Answers will vary. Sample: Effect: The cat can sneak up on the mice; Cause: The mice can't hear the cat coming; Cause: The mice are scared to go near the cat.

2. Answers will vary. Sample: No, the problem has not been solved. The idea is good, but no one wants to follow through with it.

Critical Thinking answers will vary. Sample: The old mouse shook his head sadly because he knew that it was not a workable solution.

Cause and Effect, p. 108

1. Answers will vary. Accept any three: breaking off pieces to sell or keep; dropping dynamite into the water to catch fish; polluting the water; contributing to global warming.

2. Answers will vary. Sample: Coral bleaching is the result of the world's oceans becoming warmer.

3. Answers will vary. Sample: Without coral reefs, the ocean's ecosystems will be out of balance.

Critical Thinking answers will vary. Sample: If all the coral reefs died, it would destroy the ocean's ecosystems. We rely on food from the sea, so a lot of people might end up starving.

Answer Key (cont.)

Draw Conclusions, p. 110

1. deeper; colder; lake; pond
2. Answers will vary. Sample: a pond about a quarter mile from a river: from the river overflowing its banks; a pond near a parking lot in a mall: manmade for flood control; a pond with a beaver den in the center: a beaver built a dam to block a stream

Critical Thinking answers will vary. Sample: The author thinks that springtime is the most interesting time because he or she likes how life in and around a pond starts to revive.

Draw Conclusions, p. 112

1. Answers will vary. Sample: The safest place to be during a blizzard is indoors because the wind chill outside can freeze you to death.
2. Answers will vary. Sample: The two factors that make a blizzard worse than an ordinary snowstorm are high winds and low temperatures.
3. Answers will vary. Sample: A person cannot see well enough to drive during a blizzard so he or she might run into something.
4. Answers will vary. Sample: The settlers might have been hit by a gust of wind and let go of the rope. Then they couldn't see where they were going and wandered off away from shelter.

Critical Thinking answers will vary. Sample: The storm still caused trouble because the homes were not built to withstand the weight of so much snow.

Infer, p. 114

1. two
2. Answers will vary. Sample: The bones in my foot give it shape and let me walk.
3. the thyroid bone
4. voluntary; involuntary; voluntary; involuntary; voluntary

Critical Thinking answers will vary. Sample: Identifying which muscles were voluntary and which were involuntary made me think about whether I had control over each of the muscles listed.

Infer, p. 116

1. Answers will vary. Sample: Sir Hubert is more fearful than he appears because sweat trickles down his spine and he feels a sense of panic.
2. Answers will vary. Sample: No, Princess Penelope is not aware of Sir Hubert's true feelings because he hides his feelings well.
3. Answers will vary. Sample: Because the title has the word "danger," I think that things are not what they seem so they are probably being dishonest with the princess.

Critical Thinking answers will vary. Sample: I think King Griffen will capture the princess and lock her in his tower.

Summarize, p. 118

1. Answers will vary. Sample: Main Idea: Ballet dancers are athletes who train very hard; Details: originated in Italy; French made it into what we know; ballerinas are girls; danseurs are boys; train at an early age; daily lessons; may join a professional company as teens; train very hard; have complete control over their bodies
2. Answers will vary. Sample: Although Ballet originated in Italy, the French made it into the art form we know. Ballerinas and danseurs begin training at an early age and may have daily lessons. They train very hard to make their bodies move and pose in difficult ways.

Critical Thinking answers will vary. Sample: Writing a summary of the text helped me to concentrate on its main idea because I had to decide what information is most important.

Summarize, p. 120

1. Answers will vary. Sample: Paragraph 1: Ancient Greek life centered on religion; Paragraph 2: The ancient Greeks made statues and beautiful temples for their gods; Paragraph 3: Greek plays had religious or political themes, and some are still performed today; Paragraph 4: They made advances in biology, mathematics, astronomy, and geography; Paragraph 5: Medicine was an important science for the Greeks, and they even came up with treatments for diseases.

Critical Thinking answers will vary. Sample: Summary sentences make it clear what each paragraph is going to talk about.

Answer Key *(cont.)*

Paraphrase, p. 122

1. four
2. Answers will vary. Sample: When cell phones first came out, they were expensive and big; Today's cell phones are smaller and perform more functions than just phone calls; One cell phone maker is currently working on a phone that runs on soda and would be better for the environment; The bio-battery would decay naturally and last three times longer than current cell phone batteries.
3. Answers will vary. Sample: Cell phones are more popular than landlines because they can perform multiple functions but their batteries contain toxic metals. A cell phone bio-battery is being created that would be better for the environment and last three times longer than current batteries.

Critical Thinking answers will vary. Sample: Summing up the text in my own words helped me to understand what I read because I had to decide what the overall main idea is and which details are important enough to include in the summary.

Paraphrase, p. 124

1. five
2. Answers will vary. Samples: From an early age, Roberto Clemente loved baseball; Roberto was asked to play for the Pittsburgh Pirates; Roberto was an excellent player, and his team won the World Series twice; As a champion, Roberto never forgot his fans and wanted to help the victims of a Nicaraguan earthquake. Roberto was a great man who was voted into the Baseball Hall of Fame after his death.
3. Answers will vary. Sample: Roberto Clemente started out poor, yet his passion for playing baseball brought him fame. Although he was an excellent baseball player, he was an even greater man because he lost his life while trying to help earthquake victims.

Critical Thinking answers will vary. Sample: Summing up the text in my own words made me think about what was important in the text and then decide how I wanted to say it.

Table of Contents, p. 126

1. 14 chapters (The index is not a chapter.)
2. about 150 pages
3. page 109
4. "Asian Immigration"
5. "World War II in Europe," "World War II in the Pacific," "World War II Leaders"

Critical Thinking answers will vary. Sample: A table of contents is not in alphabetical order like the index. It is a listing of the chapters in the order in which they appear in the book.

Table of Contents, p. 128

1. 11 chapters (The index is not a chapter.)
2. about 190 pages
3. page 61
4. "Joining an Existing Team"
5. "Leading the Team"

Critical Thinking answers will vary. Sample: I would use a table of contents to see what kinds of topics are covered in the book by scanning the chapter titles.

Index, p. 130

1. Answers will vary. Sample: The entries are listed alphabetically. I know because I looked at the first letters of each entry.
2. page 11
3. I would read about hornbooks.
4. page 12

Critical Thinking answers will vary. Sample: There is not an index in a fiction book because it is not filled with facts about topics that readers would need to look up.

Index, p. 132

1. The entries are listed alphabetically. I know because I looked at the first few letters of each word.
2. pages 20–21
3. I would read about the temperate forest.
4. page 22

Critical Thinking answers will vary. Sample: An index is in alphabetical order while a table of contents lists chapters in order.

Answer Key *(cont.)*

Glossary, p. 134

1. The definition of *coastal* is "located along a coast."
2. *Silt* means "particles of sediment."
3. Answers will vary. Sample: Freshwater is water from rivers and streams that has no salt in it, while groundwater is water that lies beneath the earth's surface.
4. Answers will vary. Sample: After many days of rain, I noticed that the rain had caused erosion on the hill behind my house.

Critical Thinking answers will vary. Sample: I would use a glossary to look up the definition of a content word in a nonfiction text if I couldn't figure out its meaning from context.

Glossary, p. 136

1. Answers will vary. Accept any two words from the glossary.
2. Student must write the definition for one of the two words listed in question #1.
3. automatic teller machine
4. exchange, barter

Critical Thinking answers will vary. Sample: A glossary lists the meaning of important words used in the book. The index lists these same words and tells on what pages to find them.

Contents of the Teacher Resource CD

Skill	Filename
Preview	
The Trip of a Lifetime	page008.pdf page009.pdf
Cleopatra: Queen of Egypt	page010.pdf page011.pdf
Predict	
Diego Rivera, An Eccentric Artist	page012.pdf page013.pdf
The Mysterious Maiden	page014.pdf page015.pdf
Prior Knowledge	
May the Force Be With You!	page016.pdf page017.pdf
Natural Forces: Electricity and Magnetism	page018.pdf page019.pdf
Set a Purpose	
Unseen Volcanoes Build New Land	page020.pdf page021.pdf
Niagara Falls	page022.pdf page023.pdf
Ask Questions	
School Website	page024.pdf page025.pdf
Our Energetic World	page026.pdf page027.pdf
Make Connections	
Rides to Remember	page028.pdf page029.pdf
The First Day at a New School	page030.pdf page031.pdf
Context Clues	
The Boy Who Hated Tests	page032.pdf page033.pdf
George Washington Carver	page034.pdf page035.pdf
Visualize	
Running Lobster Traps	page036.pdf page037.pdf
Sofia's Quinceañera Gown	page038.pdf page039.pdf

Skill	Filename
Story Elements	
Maritza's Dilemma	page040.pdf page041.pdf
Sleepover at the Art Museum	page042.pdf page043.pdf
Plot	
The Auto Show	page044.pdf page045.pdf
An Important Race	page046.pdf page047.pdf
Characters	
Captain Butterbeard Addresses His Crew	page048.pdf page049.pdf
King Midas's Golden Touch	page050.pdf page051.pdf
Title and Headings	
Oysterville Crate Race	page052.pdf page053.pdf
An Amazing Machine	page054.pdf page055.pdf
Typeface and Captions	
Zoos: Old and New	page056.pdf page057.pdf
Light	page058.pdf page059.pdf
Graphics	
For the Record	page060.pdf page061.pdf
Shaking and Quaking	page062.pdf page063.pdf
Topic Sentences	
Earth's Cycling Seasons	page064.pdf page065.pdf
Firefighters	page066.pdf page067.pdf
Main Idea	
Milo the Victorious	page068.pdf page069.pdf
Light Sticks	page070.pdf page071.pdf

Skill	Filename
Details	
A Giant Red Ant	page072.pdf page073.pdf
Johnson Space Center	page074.pdf page075.pdf
Main Idea and Details	
Confucius, the Great Chinese Philosopher	page076.pdf page077.pdf
Chronological Order	
The Ancient Olympics	page078.pdf page079.pdf
Thomas Jefferson	page080.pdf page081.pdf
Logical Order	
Help Nature to Recycle	page082.pdf page083.pdf
Hydroponics	page084.pdf page085.pdf
Fact and Opinion	
Change Comes to School Lunches	page086.pdf page087.pdf
Pablo Picasso	page088.pdf page089.pdf
Proposition and Support	
School Garbage	page090.pdf page091.pdf
Fighting for Survival	page092.pdf page093.pdf
Author's Purpose	
I'm Sorry	page094.pdf page095.pdf
A Visit to Saturn	page096.pdf page097.pdf
Compare and Contrast	
A Difficult Choice	page098.pdf page099.pdf
African Ecosystems	page100.pdf page101.pdf
Classify	
Taste	page102.pdf page103.pdf
At the Library	page104.pdf page105.pdf

Skill	Filename
Cause and Effect	
Belling the Cat	page106.pdf page107.pdf
Trouble in the Coral Reefs	page108.pdf page109.pdf
Draw Conclusions	
At the Pond	page110.pdf page111.pdf
Blizzard!	page112.pdf page113.pdf
Infer	
Your Skeleton and Muscles	page114.pdf page115.pdf
Danger from the Sky	page116.pdf page117.pdf
Summarize	
Ballet	page118.pdf page119.pdf
Ancient Greece	page120.pdf page121.pdf
Paraphrase	
"Green" Cell Phones	page122.pdf page123.pdf
Roberto Clemente	page124.pdf page125.pdf
Table of Contents	
The Twentieth Century	page126.pdf page127.pdf
Teamwork	page128.pdf page129.pdf
Index	
History of Schools	page130.pdf page131.pdf
Earth's Biomes	page132.pdf page133.pdf
Glossary	
Wetlands	page134.pdf page135.pdf
History of Money	page136.pdf page137.pdf

Notes

#50728—*Read and Succeed: Comprehension Level 5*